Ministry with Older Persons

Ministry with Older Persons

A Guide for Clergy and Congregations

ARTHUR H. BECKER

AUGSBURG Publishing House • Minneapolis

MINISTRY WITH OLDER PERSONS
A Guide for Clergy and Congregations

Copyright © 1986 Augsburg Publishing House

Scripture quotations unless otherwise noted are from the Revised Standard Version of the Bible, copyright 1946, 1952, and 1971 by the Division of Christian Education of the National Council of Churches.

Library of Congress Cataloging-in-Publication Data

Becker, Arthur H.
  MINISTRY WITH OLDER PERSONS.

  Bibliography: p.
  1. Church work with the aged.   2. Aged—Religious
life. I. Title.
BV4435.B37   1986   253.5'0880565   86-1101
ISBN 0-8066-2196-6

Manufactured in the U.S.A.   APH 10-4444

            4   5   6   7   8   9   0   1   2   3   4   5   6   7   8   9

To Betty,
my beloved companion
on the pilgrimage of aging

Contents

Preface

The primary purpose of this book is that the gracious promise of the gospel be personalized in communication with the older members of our society and with Christian congregations. It is the essence of pastoral care that this gospel promise first be incarnated within a caring personal relationship and then be articulated through Word and sacraments. Concern for pastoral care in this form is the central thread of this book on ministry among elders.

Many books have been published in recent years. *Aging* has become an "in" word, almost replacing society's preoccupation with "death and dying." So why still another book on the subject? Almost all the books now available look at aging from the useful perspectives of geriatric medicine, sociology, gerontology, geriatric psychology, and anthropology; few consider the spiritual or theological aspects of aging or the importance of religious issues for persons growing older. I am convinced that the pastoral care of aging persons involves more than psychological, sociological, or psychiatric understanding of the aging process. As truly helpful as these perspectives are, the aging person lives out life on additional levels. This book addresses these spiritual, theological aspects of aging in order that the ministry of the gospel among this rapidly expanding segment of our population be enhanced.

This book is written chiefly for pastors and students preparing for pastoral ministry. I do not mean, however, that this ministry should be restricted only to those who are ordained. There are many well-qualified and well-intentioned lay persons who can carry on this ministry alongside ordained pastors and under their supervision; there ought to be many more. "Pastoral" ministry is accomplished by anyone who, representing and delegated by Christian congregations or worshiping communities, seeks to personalize and articulate the promises of the gospel of grace as revealed in our Lord Jesus Christ.

This is neither a book on gerontology nor a theology of aging, though much material from both these perspectives is included. I have tried, instead, to include what I feel to be the essentials that the pastor or lay visitor may need for effective ministry to the elder saints of the community and the congregation. I write from a Lutheran perspective, though I do not feel that this is at odds with traditional, ecumenical, pastoral theology. I have at points alluded to liturgical or theological resources peculiar to Lutheranism, but similar resources exist in almost every faith community grounded in the gospel of Christ. My intent is that these rich resources be faithfully used. To all pastors I write out of the conviction that the ministry and message of the church make a contribution that no other discipline or agency can make to all who are growing older, and that this unique ministry and message become more important with the passing years.

Ministry among elders is important and will become increasingly so. By 1990 the average Christian congregation of 100 members will have 43 persons over the age of 65. Though average life expectancy has not changed a great deal in the past three decades, the number of people reaching 65 or older has increased dramatically, chiefly because of advances in health care and new medical technologies. The more effectively and faithfully we minister to this group, the more effectively we will also be serving younger people as they face the inevitability of their own aging. Older persons in our churches need the Word of grace, but they also represent a vast potential for service to the congregation and the wider community. They can be liberated for such service to church and world by faithful ministry.

This book is divided into two broad sections. The first nine chapters are concerned with understanding the aging process and elderly people. The last five chapters seek to make use of these understandings for effective ministry.

It is my hope that this book will provide helpful resources for all pastoral persons, for the encouragement and enrichment of ministry among the elder saints who surround us.

Acknowledgments

Writing a book is, in many ways, like living a life—a weaving together of many strands of interaction with other people, ideas, and experience. Both are tapestries that blend color, form, and line into a coherent whole of meaning and beauty. Central themes emerge, and a mood is created that bears the marks of significant influences or contributions from others, some of which can be identified, and others which are beyond tracing.

This book emerges at the end of a pastoral teaching career. To identify and acknowledge with appropriate thanks all the influences and contributors would be to write an autobiography. Parents and grandparents, by being gracious elders, silently taught me much that is woven into the fabric of my living, teaching, and writing. The challenging interaction with students and their lively, probing questions has enriched and called forth this writing. It is partly for them, many now pastors, and for some who will follow that this book has been written. The experiences of many of these seminary students are woven into this book as they shared their learning experiences of ministry among elders. This has done much to shape the issues and give color and life to this book.

For the patience of my wife, who gives sturdy encouragement and challenging criticism, reflective of a steadfast love, I am deeply grateful. To my children, who in youthful enthusiasm pursue their destinies and fulfill their dreams, forming a sharp contrast ld never have become words on a well-typed page without the faithful work of Mae Wagner, who, without complaint, typed pages of redrafts and was as eager as the author for the book to be well done.

There are many others—teachers, writers, fellow pastors—whose influences have been woven into the fabric of the text. I trust that they will be rewarded by whatever contribution this book may make to more effective pastoral care of the elder saints among us.

Rose, Estes Park, Colorado
Pentecost 1984

1

Myths and Realities of Aging

Peter S. is crowding 65. He and his wife live in a modest home which they own. For more than 40 years Peter has been a productive member of society, but now, as he nears 65, his job brings him less and less satisfaction. He looks ahead to retirement and becoming an unproductive member of society. His work is suffering. He has more than his share of on-the-job accidents, and his absence from work is increasing, due both to increased "sick days" and lack of motivation. Peter's boss has had to keep him on the same job that he has held for a number of years, even though he needs someone with Peter's skills on some of the newer machines that have come into the shop. The boss knows that it's difficult to retrain someone who is past 60.

Although the needs Peter and his wife have are in many ways less than when they were young, they are on the verge of becoming a drain on the country's resources. Yet after all the years of work Peter has put in, both he and his wife feel they deserve what the quiet "golden years" can bring them. As he thinks about all this, Peter gets more depressed than he used to. When he gets unusually blue, he sometimes even thinks about "ending it all."

There are few joys left for Peter. His sex life is a thing of the past, and he can't even enjoy a good meal anymore because of chronic stomach trouble. Like most people reaching 65, he is apt to forget things, make foolish remarks, and even throw temper tantrums when things don't go just right. But he is learning to accept these changes that are a part of growing older. He and his wife are backing out of life, disengaging. Both of them expect to live out the closing years of their lives in a rest home.

Uncovering the stereotypes

Peter and his wife are an imaginary couple. Their story reveals many of the stereotypes, many of them fallacies of aging. It's difficult to recognize all these myths because so many have become a part of our national consciousness (notice, for example, how older people are portrayed on television). Most of these stereotypes have little basis in reality, much like our cultural stereotypes of blacks, hispanics, and other minorities. Like racism or sexism, "agism" is a way of thinking and relating to others without taking the time or effort to view them as persons who, like ourselves, have been created in the image of God. But "agism" differs in one important respect from all the other "isms": almost all of us will eventually become its victims. Everyone who lives past the age of 60 or 65 will become subjected to the pervasive stereotypes of aging. That's one of the reasons why most of us are as afraid of growing older as we are afraid of dying.

There are three reasons why it is important for us, at the beginning of our study, to examine the myths and realities of aging.

First, accurate and truthful information about aging is important because this group of persons is now and will continue to be one of the larger groups with whom pastors will be ministering. Demographers are already projecting an "elder boom" that will occur when the "baby boomers" of the post-World War II era reach 65. By the year 2020 persons over 65 will constitute 18% of the general population. It is already true of most congregations that their "population pyramid" is "top heavy" with persons over 55.

Secondly, we need accurate information about the elderly because our attitudes are formed and affected by what we believe or know, and, in turn, our caring for others is colored by our attitudes about them.

In the following interchange we can see the effects of these attitudes on ministry. A young pastor visited a 74-year-old woman admitted to the hospital for orthopedic surgery. She was a church member, though not of the congregation of the visiting pastor. After the beginning introduction the visit continued:

Patient: You know, it is funny, but when I was a child I was always afraid of old age. Now here I am, 74 years old myself.

Pastor: What brought on your fear of old age? Is there anything in your childhood you can remember?

Patient: Yes, I was born in a small town and I remember leading those old people around because they couldn't get around too well, and I always thought I'd hate to be like that.

Pastor: Yes, old age is something we all have to face. If we want to live, we have to become old.

You can sense from the response that the pastor, too, shared the same feeling about growing old that the patient held when she was a child. For the pastor, old age was "something we have to face," and, by implication, a difficult time of struggle and pain, the inevitable result of living.

If we are fearful of old age and aging, we may avoid all but the obligatory contacts with older people—as physicians have tended to do. The National Interfaith Council on Aging reports that pastors, also, avoid ministry with elders. Work with older people is either neglected or relegated to a "visitation pastor," and it becomes a peripheral element of the parish program. We tend to avoid the aging, particularly the "frail elderly," almost as much as we avoid death and dying.

Ministers cannot adequately shepherd someone going through the dying process or care for the bereaved family without first beginning to come to terms with death and their own dying, and the same is true in ministry with and for older persons. In caring for the sick, the dying, and the aging, ministers must become "wounded healers"—"wounded" by exposing themselves in thought, fantasy, and experience to sickness, aging, and death.

There is no easy way to do this, though there are some helps available. One of these which we undertake in this chapter is to expose the fallacies, myths, and misinformation we have about

growing old and the aging. I suggest that readers begin by com-
pleting the "Inventory on Aging" in this chapter and the inventory "How Do You Feel About Growing Older?" in the Appendix.
A second way is to welcome or initiate encounters with older
persons and, by close personal contact with them, discover that
growing old does have its gains as well as its losses. Make contact
with a wide spectrum of older people. Often the pastor or the
physician's contact is with the institutionalized elder; as a result,
impressions are formed largely by the pathology of aging. Finally, learn as much as possible about the aging process by attending workshops or training sessions provided by universities,
mental-health agencies, and theological seminaries. Enter into
clinical programs for ministry to older persons provided in some
retirement centers.

A third reason why it is important to expose fallacies and in-
correct fantasies about aging has to do with our own aging process. Every one of us is familiar with the "self-fulfilling prophecy"
and its effects in life. The athlete is concerned almost as much
with attitude as with particular skill. If an athlete feels, "I don't
think I can win," that athlete knows that chances are greater that
failure will follow. In human development, too, we tend to grow
up to our expectations. Human beings are thinking, anticipating
organisms, and expectations of what will be are important factors
in what actually happens. Educators have become aware of the
"Pygmalion effect" on students: if a teacher expects that a student
will do good work, chances are greater than average that the
student will fulfill those expectations. The effect works even
more insidiously in the negative; students regarded by the teacher as slow learners, or as lazy and incompetent, often fulfill those
expectations.

If we anticipate that old age will be filled with misery, poverty,
suffering, loneliness, and bitterness, chances are greater than
average that it will be so. When negative expectations, fears,
prejudices, and stereotypes are uncovered, their insidious effect
on later life can be diminished.

Not long ago my wife and I attended a training session for
"SMART" leaders, a preretirement training program. Attending
the workshop were several couples who had already retired and

were delighted with their experience. In talking with them, discovering how they had solved their problems, finding out that many of the stereotypes and fallacies we feared were not in fact true, both of us gained a new sense of confidence as we face our own retirement.

If negative or false impressions of aging dominate our thinking, we will be more likely to engage in *denial*. Denial of the real negative aspects of aging is common in our youth-oriented society. Excessive denial is unwholesome because it prevents the denying person from facing the facts realistically and responding in appropriate ways to what is happening. It also encourages one to live in a fantasy world. Someone who is one of the "frail elderly" and undertakes to go out and play a vigorous game of tennis under the delusion that you are "only as old as you feel" may be in for a serious fracture or even a heart attack.

The healthy opposite of denial is not surrender. A careful regimen of exercise, diet, meditation, human contacts, and the maintenance of vital interests in order to minimize the negative effects of aging is not denial, but appropriate defensive behavior.

In an article in the *Gerontologist* (1979) Richard Kalish warns against a subtle reversal of the agism that we all know.[1] This "new agism" stereotypes the elderly as being helpless and dependent persons who need our services. It encourages the development of programs and services without adequate concern as to the effect these services have both on the needs of the persons being helped and on the reduction of their freedom. It has victimized countless helpees.

Kalish suggests that this new agism has generated some failure models of aging. These models include the *incompetent elder* and the *geriactivist elder*. The *incompetent* model puts down older people by saying that because they are poor, chronically ill, malnourished, lonely, or in some other tragic way affected by aging, they need the help, federal money, or advocacy programs, which we—the successful, strong, youthful—can provide for them. The important question must be asked by those of us would-be helpers, "Whose needs are we serving?" A further danger is that older people may internalize or "buy into" this incompetent elder model and consider themselves failures. This is severely damaging to the self-esteem of the persons whose self-confidence we had hoped to elevate.

The second failure model suggested by Kalish is the *geriactivist elder,* those who hold that successful aging requires that all old-sters become activists or advocates for the elderly. This, too, becomes a put-down for the elderly who have been deprived of the usual routes of being productive—and therefore worthy—in our culture. By taking on this new form of social "work righteousness," the aging activist strives to prove herself worthy of acceptance, and of course also proves that she is "aging successfully." For the geriactivist, something is assumed to be wrong with other older people

> who prefer to sit around and talk with elderly friends, or to stay at home and read, or thoroughly enjoy television, who wish to pray or meditate . . . who for whatever reasons prefer their world to be comfortably manageable, rather than stimulating, challenging and risky.[2]

Some balance, then, is needed in the way we manage the information and attitudes that we gain from examination of our own attitudes and the gathering of corrective information.

Inventory on aging

The following inventory examines the stereotypes and realities of aging. It fosters the development of accurate information, which will be helpful in removing stereotypes and in coming to terms with our own aging. This is a carefully researched inventory designed to cover the basic physical, mental, and social facts and the most common misconceptions about aging. I will reproduce it here, along with much of the commentary as printed in the *Gerontologist,* vol. 17, August, 1977.[3] Before you read further, take the time to try out the quiz. Circle T for true and F for false.

T   F   1. The majority of old people (past age 65) are senile (i.e., defective memory, disoriented, or demented).

T   F   2. All five senses tend to decline in old age.

T   F   3. Most old people have no interest in, or capacity for, sexual relations.

T F   4. Lung capacity tends to decline in old age.

T F   5. The majority of old people feel miserable most of the time.

T F   6. Physical strength tends to decline in old age.

T F   7. At least one-tenth of the aged are living in long-stay institutions (i.e., nursing homes, mental hospitals, homes for the aged, etc.).

T F   8. Aged drivers have fewer accidents per person than drivers under age 65.

T F   9. Most older workers cannot work as effectively as younger workers.

T F   10. About 80% of the aged are healthy enough to carry out their normal activities.

T F   11. Most old people are set in their ways and unable to change.

T F   12. Old people usually take longer to learn something new.

T F   13. It is almost impossible for most old people to learn new things.

T F   14. The reaction time of most old people tends to be slower than reaction time of younger people.

T F   15. In general, most old people are pretty much alike.

T F   16. The majority of old people are socially isolated and lonely.

T F   17. The majority of old people are seldom bored.

T F   18. Older workers have fewer accidents than younger workers.

T F   19. Over 15% of the U.S. population are now age 65 or over.

T F   20. Most medical practitioners tend to give low priority to the aged.

T F   21. The majority of older people have incomes below the poverty level (as defined by the Federal Government).

T F   22. The majority of older people are working or would like to have some kind of work to do (including housework and volunteer work).

T F   23. Older people tend to become more religious as they age.

T   F   24. The majority of older people are seldom irritated or
angry.
T   F   25. The health and socioeconomic status of older people
(compared to younger people) in the year 2000 will
probably be about the same as now.

What is the truth about each of these points?

1. "The majority of old people are not senile (i.e., defective
memory, disoriented, or demented). Only about 2 or 3% of persons age 65 or over are institutionalized as a result of psychiatric
illness. Thus, all the evidence indicates that there are less than
10% of the aged who are disoriented or demented. Most studies
agree that there is little or no decline with age in short-term
memory storage capacity (using the digit span test). As for long-
term memory, various community surveys have found less than
20% of the aged who cannot remember such things as the past
President of the U.S., their correct age, birthdate, telephone
number, mother's maiden name, address, or the alphabet. Thus
it is clear that the majority of the aged do not have such serious
memory defects."

Further discussion of this ussue will be provided in Chapter
4, "The Losses and Gains of Aging."

2. "All five senses do tend to decline in old age. Most studies
agree that various aspects of vision, hearing, and touch tend to
decline in old age. Some studies of taste and smell have not found
a significant decline."

3. "The majority of persons past age 65 continue to have
both interest in, and capacity for, sexual relations." Masters and
Johnson found that the capacity for satisfying sexual relations
continues into the 70s and 80s for healthy couples. This has been
corroborated by the work of Dr. Robert Butler.

4. "Lung capacity does tend to decline in old age. Vital lung
capacity . . . and maximum breathing capacity decline on the
average from age 30 onward."

5. "The majority of old people do not feel miserable most of
the time." Studies of happiness, morale, and life satisfaction either find no significant difference by age groups or find about
one-fifth to one-third of the ages score low on various happiness

or morale scales. A recent national survey found that less than a fourth of persons age 65 or over reported, "This is the dreariest time of my life" while a majority said "I am just as happy as when I was younger."

6. "Studies of various kinds of muscular strength show declines in old age compared to young adulthood, at 15 to 46%."

7. "Only 4.8% of persons 65 or over were residents of any long-stay institutions in 1970 (U.S. Census, 1970). Even among those age 75 or over, only 9.2% were residents in institutions."

8. "Drivers over 65 do have fewer accidents per person than drivers under age 65. Older drivers have about the same accident rate . . . as middle-aged drivers, but a much lower rate than drivers under 30 (National Safety Council, 1976)."

9. "The majority of older workers can work as effectively as younger workers. . . . Studies of older workers (the 12% who are able to continue employment) under actual working conditions . . . show that they perform as well as young workers, if not better. . . . When speed of reaction is important, older workers sometimes produce at lower rates, but they are at least as accurate and steady in their work as younger workers. Consistency of output tends to increase by age. . . . Older workers have less job turnover, less accidents and less absenteeism than younger workers."

10. "About 80% of the aged are healthy enough to engage in their normal activites."

11. "The majority of older people are not set in their ways and unable to change. There is some evidence that older people tend to become more stable in their attitudes, but it is clear that most older people do change and adapt to the many major events that occur in old age such as retirement, children leaving home, widowhood, moving to new homes, serious illness."

12. "Experiments have consistently shown that older people take longer than younger people to learn new material. . . . Older workers tend to take somewhat longer to learn new jobs."

13. "It is not impossible for most old people to learn new things. The same studies (cited in #12) also show that most older people can eventually learn new things about as well as younger persons, if given enough time." Other studies have shown that motivation to learn is of significant importance in older persons'

learning and that this is one reason why they do poorly in "non-sense syllable" recall tests.

14. "The reaction time of most old people tends to be slower than that of younger people. This is one of the best documented facts about the aged on record."

15. "There appears to be at least as much difference between older people as there is between people at any age level. . . . Some evidence indicates that as people age they tend to become less alike and more heterogeneous on many dimensions. One writer suggested that a group of people is like a fan; the farther away from the center (birth) you go, the greater the differences."

16. "Only 17% of persons 65 or over say 'not enough to do to keep busy' is a 'somewhat serious' or 'very serious' problem (Harris, 1975)." Most retirees I have interviewed indicate that they are "busier now than they ever were."

17. "The majority of old people are not socially isolated and lonely. About two-thirds of the aged say they are never or hardly ever lonely, or say that loneliness is not a serious problem. . . . Most older persons have close relatives within easy visiting distance and contacts between them are relatively frequent. About half say they 'spend a lot of time' socializing with friends. About three-fourths of the aged are members of a church or synagogue (Erskine, 1975) and about half attend services at least three times per month (*Catholic Digest,* 1960). Over half belong to other voluntary organizations."

18. "Older workers have fewer accidents than younger workers. . . . A study of 18,000 workers in manufacturing plants found that workers beyond age 65 have about one-half the rate of non-disabling injuries as those under 65."

19. "Only 10.3% of the population were age 65 or over in 1975 and this will probably not increase to more than 12% by the year 2000 . . . even if completed fertility drops to zero population growth levels (Current Population Survey, 1975)." More recent studies suggest that this might rise to 16% (*American Demographics Magazine,* Oct. 1979). A recent Bureau of Census estimate puts this figure at 18% by 2020 (National Academy of Sciences, 1982).

20. "Most medical practitioners tend to give low priority to the aged. A series of 12 empirical studies all found that most

medical students and doctors, nursing students and nurses, occupational therapy students, psychiatry clinic personnel, and social workers tend to believe the negative stereotypes about the aged and prefer to work with children or younger adults."

21. "The majority of persons 65 or over have incomes well above the poverty level. In 1975 there were only 15.3% of the aged below the official poverty level (about $2,400 for an aged individual or $3,000 for an aged couple). Even if the near poor are included, the total in or near poverty is only 25.4% (Brotman, 1976)." It should, however, be kept in mind that this study was made before serious inflation began to erode fixed incomes. Current data suggest that this proportion of persons in poverty over 65 is higher. Poverty figures are much higher for the rural aged and for minority aged.

22. "Over three-fourths of old people are working or would like to have some kind of work to do (including housework and volunteer work). There are about 12% of persons 65 or over who are employed, 21% who are retired but say they would like to be employed."

23. "Older people do not tend to become more religious as they age. While it is true that the present generation of older persons tend to be more religious than the younger generations, this appears to be a generational difference (rather than an aging effect) due to the older person's more religious upbringing." One wonders what will happen to those in the present generation who have not had a religious upbringing. Will they be deprived of a rich resource for the final years of life? This suggests to the pastor and other church professionals that it is unwise to count on the increased religiosity of older persons, while ministry efforts are expended elsewhere, such as on youth, young adults, or social issues.

In a sense the statistics here are a bit misleading. While it is true that oldsters do not automatically become more religious as they grow older, particularly if religiosity is measured by church attendance or other specifically "religious" activities (prayer, Bible reading, almsgiving, etc.), there is an increased sensitivity of "openness" to religious or philosophical issues. Other studies have demonstrated that increased interiority occurs as people grow older (this will be discussed more in detail in Chapters 2 and 3). Evangelism among older people may be a significant option for ministry, but it will have to be done with care, sensitivity, and correct assumptions about older persons.

24. "The majority of old people are seldom irritated or angry. The Kansas City Study found that over one-half the aged said they are never or hardly ever irritated and this proportion increased to two-thirds at age 80 or over. . . . The Duke Adaptation Study found that 90% of persons over 65 said they were never angry during the past week."

This finding, however, should not be interpreted to mean that older people are always taciturn or that they passively accept what happens to them. Particularly in the 1980s there is increasing anxiety and anger over criminal attacks on older people. What the studies do explode, however, is the stereotype of the "cranky old man" or the "bitchy old woman."

25. "The health and socioeconomic status of older people (compared to younger people) in the year 2000 will probably be much higher than now. Measures of health, income, occupation, and education among older people are rising in comparison to those of younger people . . . (Palmore, 1976)." This, of course, assumes a low or at least constant inflation rate of under 5%. This picture could change with a return of higher inflation.

2

The Pilgrimage of Aging

Life is change, as the "preacher" of the book of Ecclesiastes observed:

> For everything there is a season, and a time for every matter
> under heaven:
> a time to be born, and a time to die;
> a time to plant, and a time to pluck up what is planted;
> a time to kill, and a time to heal;
> a time to break down, and a time to build up;
> a time to weep, and a time to laugh;
> a time to mourn, and a time to dance;
> a time to embrace, and a time to refrain from embracing;
> a time to seek, and a time to lose; . . .
> a time to love, and a time to hate (Eccl. 3:1-8).

What is difficult for us sometimes, as it was for this ancient writer, is to determine the "right time." So we need the prayer of the psalmist, "So teach us to number our days that we may get a heart of wisdom" (Ps. 90:12). One of the ways we can "discern the time" in our own living, as well as for those for whom we care, is to organize the process of aging into periods or stages.

Understandings of Aging

The calendar has been influential from biblical times until the present: "The years of our life are threescore and ten, or even by reason of strength, fourscore; yet their span is but toil and trouble (Ps. 90:10). The *chronological* understanding of aging, the accumulation of year upon year, relates to the *biological* understanding of aging. Fascinating and encouraging research is going on to understand what happens at the cellular level as we grow older. A variety of theories are being investigated from "accident" or "wear and tear" theories to genetic theories that suggest a built-in time clock that sets an arbitrary limit on the number of times cells can reproduce.

Proverbial phrases such as "you are as old as you feel" or "as young as you feel" suggest the relative character of time in understanding aging. Bernice Neugarten points out that our perception of time changes as we grow older. Youth see time in future perspective—"the time ahead of me." One person said, "Before I was 35, the future just stretched forth. There would be time to do and see and carry out all the plans I had." In youth one's time may be reckoned from birthdate. In middle age there is a shift to "time left to live." Time begins to be reckoned by one's presumed "death date" rather than birthdate. The "time left" perspective becomes more acute the older one gets. Though one of the important bits of information you can have about a person is her age in years, that should never be the only information.

Equally important is the *psychological-emotional* understanding of aging. The central feature of this approach has to do with the adaptive capacities of individuals, their subjective reactions or self-awareness, and the range of attitudes or feelings about themselves and their experiences.

The psychological understanding of aging involves the systematic study of age differences in behavior and the means for modifying behavior at various age levels. The old saw "you can't teach an old dog new tricks" has been dramatically disproved by research into memory and learning. Older people can learn just as readily as can youth, but they learn differently as to speed, depth, and type of learning. Also it has been found that if one has spent a lifetime learning (and who of us has not, in some form or another?), one does not lose that capacity simply by being chronologically older.

Of special importance in the psychological understanding of aging has been recent research into that catchall term, *senility*.

Neurological, behavioral, and even dietary studies have determined that senility in many instances is not the age-related and age-caused loss of memory, logic, and orientation that is irreversible. What has been perceived and sometimes too quickly diagnosed as senility often is related to diet, sensory deprivation, and cardiovascular functioning and can be reversed when these factors are attended to. The phenomenon of true senility is quite rare. Therefore pastors and others who work with older people should be warned that people who seem disoriented should not be quickly written off as "simply senile." Most gerontologists today would prefer that the word *senile* be expunged from our vocabulary.

The stages of life

One shortcoming of most of the theories of human development is that they are very detailed through infancy, childhood, and adolescence, but tend to become sparse in adulthood, middle age, and senescence. Only recently have students of personality begun to research in some detail the processes of personality development into middle age and old age.

One of the first, and still most influential, scholars in this field was Erik Erikson, with his schema of the eight stages of life.

Erikson portrayed the process of personal development in terms of a set of polarities that reflect the ambiguities and ambivalences of living. These polarities include:

trust—mistrust
autonomy—doubt, shame
initiative—guilt
industry—inferiority
identity—repudiation and identity diffusion
intimacy and solidarity—isolation and alienation
generativity—self absorption/stagnation
integrity—despair

As individuals move or live through each of these stages, they establish some balance in the continuum between the two poles. The ideal, of course, is that individuals may, on balance, resolve the issues or crises of the particular stage. Erikson saw these stages as hierarchical, with the effective resolution of any particular stage dependent not only on healthy experience and integration within the stage, but dependent also on effective resolution of all previous stages.

In all of the stages, healthy development depends to a very great extent on salutary interpersonal relationships. These relationships take place primarily within the family circle, or with persons who are surrogates of essential familial figures, especially parental figures, in the earlier stages of life.

While on first glance it would seem that the last two of Erikson's stages relate particularly to older adult life, this is deceptive. Effective aging really involves all of the stages. Integrity—the sense of who one is, the feeling that life has been significant and useful (regardless of economic or social success), and that one can look back on life with minimal regret and with a contentment—is in fact the culmination of healthy resolution of all previous stages.

Erikson's schema also reveals that some central issues of life are encountered again and again, so that the entire schema might better be understood as an ascending spiral, rather than a staircase. These recurring issues are (1) basic trust (or faith)—with mistrust and anxiety the other pole, (2) resolution of the independence/self-sufficiency—dependency/interdependence issues, and (3) a sense of one's own integrity and identity. These three issues in Erikson's schema recur at more complex levels several more times in life after infancy: in adolescence, in marriage (if one marries), at what some scholars have called the mid-life crisis, again at retirement, and possibly again as one faces death. If one has in infancy and early childhood discovered that the care and love of other human beings can be depended on, regardless of whether or not one performs precisely according to their wishes and demands, this same footing for life can be of tremendous importance in facing the issue of retirement or old age. Likewise with the issue of independence, self-sufficiency, and interdependence; discovering that one can be cared for and helped as a child without loss of one's integrity and identity can be a very helpful, or even necessary, prelude to being helped and cared for as an elder.

Erikson's schema was developed in the 1950s and has held up very well as a model for investigators in the field of human development. More recently, the work of Levinson, Neugarten, and others suggests that the latter two of Erikson's stages may apply for longer periods than he first suggested. For example, he considered generativity the primary task of middle age—the period between 40 and 55. I suggest that this may be a bit too early as a beginning for this stage, and that it lasts well into what had at his time been considered "old age" (65 +). It seems to me that generativity is also a significant aspect of the years from 60-70, continuing in its waning stages beyond that time.

Let me consider an "elder" who illustrates this point. John L. is now 64, the senior partner in a business which he developed in mid-life after a financially disastrous bankruptcy of a construction business. For many years he worked at a junior-executive level in another company in order to personally repay all the creditors resulting from this bankruptcy. He was able, finally, to develop enough capital to venture into his own business once again. Now he serves as a mentor for the junior partner in the firm, sharing his experience, teaching, encouraging, and supporting the younger man. He fulfills some of these same functions in his church life as well. He has served as chairman of the congregation and its treasurer and continues to serve on the church council. He is a strong supporter of the pastors. He is farsightedly concerned about the future of his congregation and of the church at large. As health permits, there is every indication that he will continue in this clearly generative function for several years. He fulfills these same functions in his family of several children and now grandchildren. In addition to this, he occupies a sort of "patriarchal" position in the extended family, being constantly concerned about the welfare of the extended family, visiting them frequently, and often being visited by them. Anne L., like her husband, is actively involved with the church, with a vitality that belies her age. She is one of the outstanding hostesses in the congregation and is regularly involved in caring for nearby grandchildren while their mother works.

One finds couples like this in almost all congregations; they are the senior partners of many firms; they serve on boards and key committees of many community agencies and health and welfare institutions. In such people one sees generativity in a rich form.

Out of this kind of generativity develops the integrity that Erikson sees as the closing developmental phase of life. If one were to substitute a religious term for integrity, the word *hope* seems best. It is the achievement of a sense of contentment with one's life and one's future in death. It is beautifully expressed in Paul's letter to his friends in Philippi. Writing from prison, he knew he was at the end of his life (whatever his age might have been). He wrote not as the apostle who founded the congregation, but as their friend and father in Christ, to friends whom he deeply loved. "I have learned, in whatever state I am, to be content. I know how to be abased, and I know how to abound. . . . I can do all things in him who strengthens me" (Phil. 4:11-13). Here we see generativity merging into what Erikson calls "integrity," the acceptance of one's life cycle and all the people who have become significant in it as "good." Integrity expresses the wisdom that though there are "if only's" in life, they are not debilitating centers of regret and remorse. There is the recognition that the past cannot be altered, though one's attitudes about it can be.

Facing death with hope and integrity is the significant crowning achievement of the human life cycle. It is, in a certain sense, the ultimate point toward which all spiritual life, pastoral care, and the nurture of congregational life are directed. The respected theologian and pastor Albert Outler reflected:

> I guess one of the most interesting moments was when I put almost the last touch on the main draft of the four volumes of Wesley's sermons, I thought to myself, now no matter what happens, here is the job—and the most important job that I would like to leave done—done. So I have not feared death so much as feared what it would do to these interlocking projects. . . . Now the question is how much more is there to be done that I could do. That doesn't seem to matter an awful lot. . . . I thought I would have a priority of things that I would like to get done before I die. I guess I do in a vague sort of way, but no longer with a sense of urgency.[1]

Integrity is the sense of fulfillment or completeness about life, particularly about one's own life, which generates the contentment of which Paul speaks. One can lay it all in God's hands and receive the gift of hope in life through death.

There is much glib talk about these days about facing death with equanimity, dignity, and integrity, but there is nothing easy or wonderful about facing death. "Death is the ultimate thief," as a good friend told me once, comforting me at the loss of a family member. Outler said, "Death is the ultimate deprivation." Facing the awfulness of it with integrity and the courage that through it can come the fulfillment of the promises of a "new" life in God, is the hope of the Christian faith.

The dark side of integrity is despair that the one and only lifetime one has been given has been squandered, its potential unfilled, and its relationships soured. Often this leads to endless ruminating over one's past, a futile effort to change what cannot be changed, or seeking forgiveness for past wrongs.

Another scholar whose research among 40 men across a broad spectrum of life-styles and professions has had a significant impact on the understanding of the developmental aspects of aging is Daniel Levinson, chief author of *The Seasons of a Man's Life*. He does not develop a consistent "stage theory" like Erikson and others, but he does identify several significant periods of life, particularly from productive young adulthood to old age. Like most other recent scholars, he does not detail the period from 65 on, and he recognizes that further research must be done.

For our purposes, the aspects of Levinson's schema that are useful are those from what he calls "mid-life transition" onward to late adulthood.

Age 45 Mid-life Transition
_____

50 Entering Middle Adulthood
_____

60 Late Adult Transition
_____

65 Late Adulthood
_____

Levinson cautions that the five-year increments are not to be taken too literally but are, as with all chronological designations in stage theories, only approximations. Of particular interest to pastors and others who care for elders are Levinson's comments about the "four tasks of mid-life transition," which we shall examine in more detail in another chapter. The value of Levinson's work is that it focuses on developmental processes of later life. As he himself notes, there is need now for continued developmental research of the two and sometimes three decades of life that continue on beyond retirement, known as "old age." Until just recently this period has been considered as a single developmental phase or, if Erikson's generativity stage is seen to continue beyond retirement, perhaps as two phases. There is considerable evidence building that development and growth continue beyond retirement, into old age and up until death.

Three phases of old age

Most people in our culture today tend to think of old age as a single longer period of life—ranging somewhere from 65 (maybe 70) to the age of death, whatever that may be, often a span of 20 years or more. This is a rather shortsighted view that does not face the vast differences in age, life-style, and perspective that occur in this relatively long period of life. It is probable that this lumping together of all old people into one group is a part of the pervasive agism that tends to regard all older people as relatively the same.

It seems to me that the span of life from 65 to 85 or to death comprises three distinct periods. For want of a better set of labels, I am going to call them simply the *young old*, the *middle old*, and the *frail elderly*. It is hazardous to attach calendar years to these periods, but in order to arrive at some kind of differentiation, it is perhaps necessary to do so.

Let me suggest then that one might regard the *young old* to be those who are 65 to 73 years in age, give or take up to five years. The young old are the newly retired who are still very much in the prime of life, although they are no longer engaged in full-time productive careers or occupation. They are still very vigorous and want to be active in the community, in the family, in the world, and in the church. They retain this vigor in large measure by virtue of the continuation of opportunities for them to be of service in church, society, and family, and by virtue of continuing health and financial stability. Those three factors will to a large extent determine how long this period will last. Some people retain this healthful vigor until they are 80. Others lose it at age 68. So it is hazardous to attach particular age labels to this first period.

When I think of the *middle old*, those aged 73 to 80, I think of an aunt and an uncle of mine who still maintain their home in an apartment and spend all of their summers in a home in the Rocky Mountains. My uncle is a retired pastor. My aunt had her own career as a teacher, a mother and homemaker, a librarian, and as executive secretary for the Florence Crittenden Association. They have been retired since age 65. For a long time they were active in the life of the church and the life of the community, but now they have pretty well phased out of that, basically for health reasons. Yet they maintain two homes. They are still vital and alive and do not require hospitalization, though they have certainly slowed down in life and no longer ask us to go with them on two- or three-mile hikes. Both of them survived minor heart attacks, and my aunt carries a pacemaker. Yet they are both still very functional, very much alive and active. They are still *middle old*, but as both of them are now around 80 years old, they soon will be entering the third stage of old age—that of the *frail elderly.*

The *frail elderly* are those whom we tend to think of when we accept the stereotypes of old age. They comprise most of the five percent of the population over 65 who live in nursing homes. They comprise the group that requires extensive hospitalization or medical care and who no longer can maintain their own households in safety. They may have intermittent periods of health and serious degenerative illnesses. They include all of those whom we see sitting and staring vacantly into space in the hallways of care centers. One can no longer look to them for active physical participation in life, though many of them may remain mentally active, alert, and alive. One should be very careful not to characterize this group as "senile." The frail elderly are just what the label suggests, those who are *frail* for a variety of reasons.

When I think of the frail elderly, I think of my wife's mother at age 86, living in a rest home in Iowa. She was perfectly content to have others provide for all her meals and to take care of the daily, routine decisions of life. She was not in ill health, though she had a prosthesis in her hip joint and was not what we could call well, either. Though not bedridden, she was not vigorously active any longer.

Each of these three levels of aging contains particular agendas or developmental tasks that persons accomplish in the pilgrimage of life. Each of these three stages of life also present us with particular relational problems, health problems, perspective problems, and, not the least, theological or faith problems.

Some cautions

We are not suggesting that the three categories of *young old, middle old,* and *frail elderly* are an inexorable set of stages through which every adult must go according to a rigid chronological, physiological, or spiritual scheme. Evidence for this caution is readily available in most any parish where some folks of 85 are still very much *middle old* while others, at 62, are already very *frail.*

Everyone over age 62 is not the same as everyone else over 62. Elder adults are distinctive and individual, yet they do share common experiences and characteristics that set them apart from young or middle-aged folk. Social scientists use the term "age cohorts" to designate these groupings. People belong to the same age cohort who share a similar age span (perhaps 7-12 years), similar psychological awareness of life and experience, and common sociocultural or historical experiences. For example, the age cohort I am designating as *middle old* not only shares a similar age grouping (73-80), but they also had the experience of being adolescents, engaged in the task of establishing ego identity, during the Great Depression. Sharing in the challenges and stresses of that era in one of the most formative periods of life has indelibly shaped their perspectives on self and society and life. Members of this age cohort may be financially very careful, not because they are "tightwads" but because of early experiences of great economic deprivation. They may be politically conservative, not because they are socially insensitive but because they realized the importance of individual effort and ingenuity. They may be politically liberal because they discovered and perhaps experienced the importance of being supported by the society at a time when individual effort and ingenuity were fruitless because of complete lack of economic opportunities. Similarly, the age cohorts of persons 30-40 share the resistance to political and social institutions and the rebellion against authority generated by the culturally disastrous Vietnam war. As a consequence of their early adolescent experience, many people from this age cohort participate in the drug culture and culture of sexual promiscuity with its biological hazards.

The three developmental phases of aging that I have suggested provide a helpful means of identifying and locating older persons. There is a danger, of course, that these phases become "file drawers" into which people are dropped to oblivion. But the conscientious pastor or lay visitor can be helped by these distinctions, which remind us that someone who is 86 has different issues of life to deal with than someone who is 66. Knowing some of these general characteristics of the issues confronting each age cohort can be helpful in establishing an initial sensitivity to the person, as she or he lives out the pilgrimage of aging.

3

The Tasks of Aging

Most of us cannot keep up with all the research in gerontology, but we do have a special concern: understanding as deeply as we can the interior spiritual and emotional process of aging.

The concept of *individuation,* developed decades ago by Carl Jung and taken up more recently by Levinson and his associates, is a particularly helpful concept, both for aging persons and for pastors and others who care for elders. Jung thought of individuation as the flowering of what we now call the personality; it was the particular agenda and outcome of elderhood, which included a significant dimension of spiritual development. Levinson sees "the mid-life crisis" as the high point of the task of individuation. He sees this as the spiritual resolution of four polarities:

1. the young-old
2. the creation-destruction
3. the masculine-feminine
4. the attachment-separation (or intimacy-alienation)

From observation, personal experience, and working with a number of elders, both men and women, it is my feeling that these four agendas are significant, not only for the mid-life crisis, but for retirement, which can be seen as the entry point into elderhood. Moving through this "passage" of retirement involves significant psychological and spiritual tasks, which include finding one's new identity as an older person and reexamining personal identity and meaning. The concept of individuation seems to embrace these tasks and extend our understanding to include other issues involved in becoming a creative, generative older person.[1]

Let us examine each of these issues in some detail as they are initiated in the mid-life crisis and come to ascendance again at retirement.

We do not resolve, once and for all, the particular tasks of a development period, but we return to them again and again in an ascending spiral; we rework them at a deeper, or at least different, level as we move through the life cycle. This seems to be particularly true of these issues of individuation, which are but the reworking of lifetime issues involved in becoming a mature person.

1. The young—old polarity

At age 50 or 55, and once more at retirement, a person must come to terms with "growing old." In our culture being old is "a social problem," as Martin Marty has noted.[2] We resist becoming old or being identified as old or even middle-aged. At mid-life (45-55), the individual still feels young in many respects but is also increasingly confronted with the limitations of age. A woman may want to play a vigorous game of tennis and be able to, but ends up with terribly sore muscles the next day. A man may want to play volleyball with the "kids" and does so, but nurses sprains and strains as a consequence. In our economy, built on obsolescence, the stakes are quite high in this struggle to maintain youth and stave off being old. Our fascination with cosmetic approaches to maintaining some ideal age offers evidence of this struggle. When this struggle enters its second round, at or about the time of retirement, it has a slightly different dimension. At the mid-life crisis the struggle was to keep up with the youngsters in the firm, in the classroom, or wherever one has lived and worked. One needed to do this to maintain one's position in the economic, social, and community structures. At this point one experiences a "marginality" similar to that experienced in adolescence, when one was neither child nor adult. Now one is neither young adult, middle-aged, nor old.

At retirement, keeping up with the youngsters is no longer the issue. One is leaving the world of economic productivity to enter a new kind of productivity—not vocational or economic productivity, but a "spiritual productivity." The person is concerned with the productivity Erikson referred to with his term *generativity:* becoming a good mentor, a bearer of tradition, a wise elder who can give guidance when asked (although this may be more rarely than the elder wishes). The elder engages in two somewhat distinct movements, a selective *interaction* and a selective *disengagement.*

There is a *disengagement* from the stress of economic and occupational concerns in order to permit one's own religious sense—the search for ultimate meanings—to develop as fully as possible. In psychological terms this disengagement allows for the reentry into awareness of some of the deeply buried memories of the past, a reworking of old wounds, a deeper encounter with one's own unconscious and the archetypal images of the folk and race. Disengagement also allows the person to use time to cultivate and deepen friendships and develop alternate vocational and leisure activities.

This leads almost inevitably to a selective *interaction* in some specialized areas. There may be an intensification of activity in interpersonal relations and in specific types of productivity. This may be a postretirement career, to maintain a sense of self-esteem and to allow for the gradual, rather than sudden, loss of the all-important job identity.

These processes are particularly evident in the earlier years of old age and diminish as the person becomes older, less capable of activity, and more subject to the normal degenerative processes.

2. The creation-destruction polarity

The second of the polarities the newly retired person must work through, and at a deeper level than at the mid-life crisis, is the creation-destruction or mortality-immortality polarity. In the mid-life crisis, the person is coming to terms with being at the peak years of occupational, vocational, and parental creativity—a member of the "dominant age cohort." One comes to terms with personal impulses of competition and even destruction— the "killer instinct" of the aggressive executive, for example. In so doing, the person realizes that she has both hurt and helped others—done hurtful things to parents, children, and rivals, as well as aided them by one's successes and by one's nurturing. A need for special forgiveness and reconciliation may emerge, calling for pastoral care.

In the mid-life crisis the person comes to terms also with her impulses to be creative. The individual feels the pressure of "so little time left" to complete the dream of life, whatever that may be—whether perfect children, a successful career, or a significant artistic achievement. The image of the "legacy" is potent in mid-life, as well as in later life.

These same themes come up again for consideration at retirement. Only now there is a slightly different twist. The polarity of creation-destruction takes on more of the emphasis of mortality-immortality, living and dying. Living becomes somewhat pressurized, as one now engages in the spiritual assessment of the individuation process and considers once again how one has done irrevocably hurtful things to parents, to children, to spouse, friends, and rivals. A profound sense of guilt may become pervasive, and this is of particular concern for the pastor. Now that the pressures of occupation and parenthood are relived, there may be renewed concern for reconciliation and for repair of those relationships that have been damaged by one's destructive impulses and life-style.

On the *creativity* side of the polarity, the elder must now come to terms with transmutations of creativity, since the avenues of occupation or wage earning are no longer available. Now new and significant opportunities for work must be found, avenues by which the elder can still make contributions to the common welfare. As Bianchi notes, "While there is great value for the elderly . . . in pursuing inner psychological and spiritual goals away from total immersion in the work world, we also need meaningful options for continuing participation in the labors of society."[3] From a theological point of view, the elder is still being called on by God to participate in God's creation; significant work makes one a participant both in continuing creation and in the providence of God for others.

The ultimate aspect of this polarity is, of course, coming to terms with death and the Christian hope. The encounter with death goes through peaks and valleys in the human life cycle; one of those peaks is at adolescence, occuring as youthful fascination with death and sometimes, tragically, as suicide. Another of the peaks occurs at the mid-life crisis, especially in the form of concern for time to complete one's life work or destiny. This concern peaks once again at retirement and finally during the last stage of old age as one is dying. Without this recurring encounter with mortality, potential for deeper spiritual growth is lessened. The positive traits of growing old—maintaining youthful perspective and vitality, continuing interest in relationships— are but a sham if they are used to deny the reality of one's mortality. Joseph Sittler has observed that we are instructed in the inevitability of our own death by the "little deaths" in our personal world.[4] This, too, is a significant area for pastoral care and guidance.

3. The masculine-feminine polarity

A third polarity that comes into sharp focus during the mid-life crisis and again at the entry into elderhood is the continuing struggle with one's "gender balance." For men this means coming to terms with the feminine as well as the masculine; for women it means dealing with the aggressive, wish-to-dominate side of one's personality, which a male-oriented culture has frequently had to be denied by women. It was Carl Jung who in the early decades of this century noted that every person is a particular and unique balance of the male and the female, elements which have often been perceived in terms of cultural stereotypes. It is difficult to talk about this balance and the shifts that take place in aging without recourse to those stereotypes. In general this aspect of human personality has to do with aggressiveness/dominance and submissiveness/passivity drives and with tenderness and compassion in contrast to objectivity and detachment in dealing with others.

It is commonly recognized in the literature on aging that as men grow older, impulses of tenderness and compassion become more dominant, coming into balance or even taking the ascendancy over "typical male" impulses of objective rationality, "business is business" attitudes. A male-oriented culture such as ours has established what Ian Suttie called "a taboo on tenderness"; this taboo begins to be shattered at the mid-life crisis and crumbles at entry into elderhood. The more nurturing (presumably female or maternal) characteristics in the man come to the fore and bid for recognition. This may be a part of grandfathering, whether literally or culturally.

For women there is a similar shift; the cultural taboo against aggressiveness deteriorates as women reach the peak of occupational or vocational activity in the work force. It has been suggested that these impulses are released particularly after the literal task of mothering is completed and mothers face the "empty nest" and seek alternate or successive careers. Women, it is suggested, now are free to recognize the more rational/managerial side of their nature; they are free to become more intrusive and aggressive, rather than assume the passive roles demanded by a male-oriented culture.

David Gutman (1975) had proposed a family life cycle in which, in early phases of life, both sexes are involved in acquiring characteristics essential to parenthood, the establishment of trust in others, the attainment of reliable inner controls, and training the executive capacities of the ego. The narcissism of youth is transformed by parenthood into nurturance, the woman sometimes nurturing both children and husband. As the responsibilities of parenthood decrease, women are free to express the "typically male" characteristics of aggressiveness, dominance, and the exercise of authority. A rather interesting evidence of this is to note how many women drive cars in which older couples are riding, as compared to the prevalence of male drivers among young couples. These trends continue until a "normal androgyny" of later life occurs, the tendency of both sexes to become more like each other.

Research suggests that both sexes, after brief dislocation, accommodate to this greater freedom to express the full range of hitherto submerged aspects of the self. Men become more sensual, openly dependent, openly tender—and without apology; women become happily active, less needful of affection and support, more willing to take risks. These shifts can lead to new capacities for enjoyment, new sensitivities to others, for both men and women.

An aspect of sexuality that must not be overlooked is genital sexuality. Until Butler wrote his book *Sex After Sixty* several years ago, it was commonly thought that older people did not continue to enjoy the physical aspects of sexual intimacy. One of the myths of agism is that of "dirty old man" and "dried-up old maid." Much of the sexual humor dealing with aging is cruel, inaccurate, and usually not funny, particularly to older people. As one elder put it, "After you reach a certain age, you discover that most jokes about aging aren't funny anymore." It is rather interesting, if not ironic, that most of the humor about old age does deal with sexuality, or the assumed impossibility of it.

The fact is that sexual interest and capability, at varying levels of sexual expression, may continue until the 90s. Masters and Johnson have contended, "There are only two basic needs for regularity of sexual expression in the 70-80-year-old woman; these are a reasonably good state of health and an interested and interesting partner." The style of sexual intimacy may change. As one elderly couple put it, "The sex life of older married couples is not confined to the bedroom." As the male ages, he finds that orgasm may become less desirable and may require more time and stimulation than formerly. But if the man and woman both understand this, then sexual interaction, which might include activities in addition to coitus, between older married partners can take place with mutual enjoyment, warmth, and fulfillment.

Pastors need to be aware of the possibilities for continuing sexual fulfillment in order to provide support, encouragement, and sanction for these activities when the appropriate opportunity arises. In the event of the remarriage of a widow or a widower, the pastor may be called upon to interpret these needs to younger children. Paradoxically, it is often the children who are opposed to such marriage out of lack of understanding of the continuing needs of older people for affection and love, sexually expressed.

Many of the stereotypes regarding senescent sexuality are generated by traditional, moralistic attitudes that sex is "dirty." Current attitudes and practices around sexuality, particularly by the young, are paradoxically beginning to generate similar attitudes, in spite of our much vaunted "sexual freedom." Another source of these attitudes, I suspect, has to do with more deeply held archetypes related to the family dynamics of early childhood. Most of us, I suspect, can still recall our shock when, as children or adolescents, we discovered that our parents "did it." And for similar reasons even we adults are a little shocked to think that grandparents "do it."

For the current age cohort of persons 70 or over, frank discussion of sexuality may be distasteful or held to be socially or morally unacceptable. The pastor and other gerontologists need to be sensitive to this. They should also tread with great sensitivity when they counsel marriages or single individuals in these matters. Care must also be exercised not to make older persons for whom direct sexual expression is no longer a continuing interest or need feel guilty, just as one must be careful about making those whose sexual interest is still lively feel guilty.

Consider the 72-year-old widow who had periodic abdominal distress but upon physical examination was found to be healthy. Finally, alone with her doctor, she tearfully confessed. Her conscience was troubled because she had been having dreams every night that her late husband was returning to her. In the dreams he frequently made love to her, and she found the sexual relation completely satisfying. She had a deep sense of guilt for this continuing sexual interest. She feared that her unmarried daughter might find out about her "disgrace." She was told that her experience was one of the "normal possibilities." It was difficult for her to accept this at first, but as she was able to, her symptoms disappeared.

Old notions about the female menopause being a catastrophic event in the lives of women have been found, on the basis of recent research, to be largely unfounded. Bernice Neugarten, one of the foremost gerontology researchers of the 1980s, concluded after her research on the subject, "Women generally feel better after the menopause than they felt in years."[5] Sixty-eight percent of the women in her study, between ages 45-65, agreed to this statement. Twenty-one percent of the older women "felt that a woman is concerned about how her husband will feel toward her after menopause," and 21% of the women between 56-65 agreed that "after menopause a woman is more interested in sex than she was before." Older women seem to feel more confident and free, the loss of fertility being of far less concern than was formerly thought.

Regular sex expression is not only possible but desirable, because, along with physical well-being and a healthy attitude toward the aging process, it provides a sexually stimulating climate within the marriage, a context for sexual enjoyment lasting well beyond the 80-year mark.

4. *The intimacy-alienation polarity*

Intimacy-alienation (or attachment-separation) at the mid-life crisis and its repetition at the point of retirement is really an update of the same crisis encountered in late adolescence. There are strong forces at play that can generate a greater degree of distancing or isolation, and another set that impels toward greater intimacy and attachment.

To most younger persons infected with the agism of our culture, old age appears as a time of diminishment, degeneration, illness, and isolation. Pressures toward age segregation in housing and social structures contribute to this separation of younger persons from elders. When old age is perceived as something undesirable and miserable, then those who fear becoming old distance themselves from those who already "have the disease," just as we almost instinctively tend to avoid persons who are seriously ill or dying. As the elders move on toward death, this ostracism may increase, unless specific steps are taken to counteract it. Agism does not simply come from the broader culture; it is also the reflection of our avoidance of that which we fear— growing older. In a study done in Waverly, Iowa, in which Pastor Larry Trachte interviewed residents of nursing homes, many said that the nursing homes resembled concentration camps, places where society sends surplus or unproductive population: "They are our way of not having to confront the aged."[6]

Other forces, part of the normal developmental process, also contribute to the isolation of elders. Departing from, or being removed from, significant social and economic roles isolates the elder from work mates and colleagues.

Another factor which tends to isolate is economic. Studies have found that, contrary to popular belief, elders do not attend church with greater frequency as they grow older. On the contrary, in many instances church attendance drops off. One of the reasons is economic: elders, particularly those below the poverty level, feel they do not have adequate "dress-up" clothing to wear. One must remember that the current cohort of elders was taught that one dresses up to go to church. A further reason is the shame attached to not having enough money to put into the offering plate. We may deplore this and regard it as unnecessary, but for many elders it is significant. Not being able to keep pace with the social group of which one was a part during economically productive wage-earning days is a related factor here. As inflation continues to erode established pension plans or other entitlement programs, these economic forces contributing to isolation and alienation are likely to increase.

For economic reasons, older persons may have to change their place of residence, resulting in the loss of neighborhood support and friends.

But it is at the time of retirement that the intimacy-isolation issue must be faced in a manner that strongly influences attitudes about one's self and one's life-style. At that point one prepares to reap the harvest of the relationships and skills one has developed or failed to develop earlier in life. This can bring both significant threat or blessing. Social, community, kinship, and congregational support can be vital at this time.

The same forces that contribute to isolation and separation can also assist in the development of greater intimacy and attachment. These, along with other aspects of individuation at the mid-life crisis and at the entry into elderhood, can contribute to a richer and more satisfying life-style than had been previously known. The same pressures that tend toward age segregation can also assist in establishing a new network of friends and associates among one's age cohorts. Particularly in retirement communities, the level of social interaction and friendship networks is significant and often higher than that found among pre-retirees. In later life one enters more clearly defined age cohorts and thus finds friendship possibilities that are not simply dependent upon one's work or profession. The research does indicate, however, as a general rule women, both married and single, have a higher level of social interaction and derive greater satisfaction from friendship-interaction. A somewhat tragic observation of Levinson's highlights a real need area: "Friendship was largely noticeable by its absence . . . close friendship with a man or a woman is rarely experienced by an American man." At the mid-life crisis and again at retirement, the male in particular should concentrate on establishing friendships that are not restricted to business associates.

The concept of *individuation* and the tasks that this involves can be significant in understanding both the developmental processes and the dynamics of aging. It is helpful not only at the time of mid-life crisis, as Levinson suggests, but also in coming to terms with one's own aging and the understanding of older persons generally, as Jung maintained. Individuation has physical, psychological, social, and spiritual implications of considerable importance to pastoral ministry with older persons. It can help the pastor or lay minister understand aging parishioners and be sensitive to when they may need special pastoral or congregational support.

4

The Losses and Gains of Aging

If most people were asked to draw the lifeline of a human being, I suspect that it would look rather like a mountain. One would start at the ground level of birth, ascend into the foothills of childhood, climb the rocky slopes of adolescence, and finally arrive at the peak of maturity and productivity to enjoy the blessings of respect, income, family, and parenthood. At mid-life, having reached the peak, the lifeline would go downhill on the other side, through the rocky valley of illness, through the dark forests of fear and loneliness into old age, and finally to ground level again, into death.

Though in some respects this might be an accurate picture, it also reveals the stereotypes of agism. For some, life is indeed like this. For others, the path into old age is not a path of descent, but of continued growth in a variety of ways; the peak becomes a large plateau, prior to further ascent into new heights. The aging years are neither all bleak nor all golden. It is more helpful for those who minister to older people to have a realistic perception of what is involved in becoming older: it is a mixed bag of gains and losses, of bad news and good news.

Physical losses

In a helpful article, "Aging: Downward, Upward, or Forward?" Paul Pruyser called attention to this complex of gains and losses in aging, suggesting that the "bell curve" of ascent and

descent is only one of the several lifelines that describe aging.[1]
The mountain journey we have outlined above is probably most
appropriate for depicting *physical* aspects of aging, for there is a
clearly discernible process of growth and development reaching
a peak and then a fairly typical degenerative path, which for the
average American man looks similar to this:

> Age 30: In most ways he is at his peak, the tallest, strongest, and
> maybe the smartest he has ever been. And yet he can see the first
> lines on his forehead. He can't hear quite as well as he could. His
> skull's circumference has started swelling. His degeneration has be-
> gun.
>
> Age 40: He's an eighth of an inch shorter than he was ten years
> ago, and each hair follicle has thinned two microns, but not every-
> thing is shrinking; his waist and chest are ballooning. All over he's
> begun to feel the weight of time's passage; his stamina is greatly
> diminished.
>
> Age 50: His eyes have begun to fail him, particularly at close range.
> He notices quirky changes; his speaking voice has risen from a C
> to an E-flat, his thumbnails are growing more slowly, and his erec-
> tions have dipped below the horizontal mark.
>
> Age 60: By now he has shrunk a full three-quarters of an inch. He
> has trouble telling some colors apart, distinguishing between high
> tones, making distinctions among the different foods he tastes. His
> lungs take in just about half what they would have 30 years ago.
>
> Age 70: His heart is pumping less blood. His hearing is worse, and
> his vision weakening. Yet if he's made it this far, say the statistics,
> he will live another 11 years. And if he has the right attitude, he
> will look back with awe at the wonders that have made him what
> he has become.[2]

Two areas of physical loss have special implications for ministry. Both have to do with sensory changes. As one grows older,
there is a subtle change in the ability to hear. Most individuals
over 40 experience some loss of high tone perception. High-
pitched voices are more difficult to hear, which may be of concern
to pastors with higher-pitched voices. There is also a greater
tendency for men than for women to experience impaired hearing as they grow older. These changes explain why persons with
some hearing loss find it easier to understand male voices or
lower-pitched voices, and why trying to speak louder is of little

help, because as we yell, we pitch our voices higher. Speaking more slowly and lowering the pitch would be far more effective. P.A. systems in churches should also be tuned very carefully to maximize perception.

Loss of hearing sets up a vicious circle. The individual with considerable hearing loss compensates for the difficulty by denial or bluffing (giving the impression that she hears and understands when she doesn't) or withdrawing from situations in which hearing and perception is required. Both of these moves tend to isolate the person from other people, thus contributing further to the denial, and, because of lessened use of the impaired ability, the loss becomes even greater.

Related to hearing, because it is also controlled in the inner ear, is the matter of balance and dizziness for older people. Body sway tends to increase with age, and dizziness may be related to hearing loss.

There is a similar change in taste sensitivity. After the late 50s, there is a decline in sensitivity due to a decline in the number of taste buds, which also accounts for a loss in capacity to discriminate between tastes.

Changes in sight are similar to changes in hearing. There is a gradual clouding of the retina so that, for those affected (usually after age 70), it appears as though one were looking at the world through translucent wax paper. There is also a gradually lowering threshhold of light sensitivity; older people require more light for reading. Contrast discrimination also changes with age; one is less able to distinguish between various shades of colors—particularly blue and green. These findings have safety implications all the way from the design of church stairways and entrances to driving at night and the scheduling of church meetings.

Older persons are generally slower to respond to most sources of stimulation. This may be due either to the fact that elders are more cautious and wish to review the stimulus before responding or that the inability of sensors to provide the central nervous system with the same amount of excitation-energy as formerly requires more time to achieve discrimination of the stimulus. Probably both factors are involved. Evidence suggests that age 70 is a threshhold at which sensory processes frequently become a more serious limiting factor for an individual. Sensory changes and losses after that age tend to become more rapid and sharply evident. It should be kept in mind, however, that prior experience, level of education, general capacity for adaptation, and compensation can significantly modify these effects.

An emotional response related to the losses of sensory and physiological characteristics is of particular importance to the pastor. It has to do with change in one's "body image." The only other time in life where one's body image was so important was in adolescence, when the body image was assaulted by the changes of puberty. At that time, growing required an adjustment from less to more—more body fat, more curves for girls, more hair, more muscles for boys, and, for both sexes, more impulse or vitality, not only in sexuality but in vigor and ambition for life. Now, in what has been called *senescence,* growing requires coming to terms with the change from more to less—less muscle, fewer curves, or at least change in them, loss of hair, loss of vitality, some loss in sexual impulse, along with loss of certain forms of sexual capacity. Wrinkles, graying or whitening hair, loss of teeth, the necessity for glasses, a cane, a crutch, support hose, or other prostheses now available—all bring about a change in body image.

If one's self-worth and self-concept have depended on how beautiful one appeared, then aging can come as a profound shock. Every aging person struggles with the impact of reduced attractiveness—on how others regard one and how we regard ourselves. Change in body image also brings changes in self-concept—how we think about ourselves. A new, more secure base for self-esteem has to be fashioned.

Loss of social role

Perhaps the most pervasive loss in aging in the social domain is the loss of a significant social role upon retirement. Several facets of social role must be taken into consideration. These include the work role, economic role, familial role, and community roles. All of these involve issues of productivity, "worth," and social, economic, or moral power.

In part, loss of social role is class related, having a significant impact on people in the white-collar or middle-management realm. Yet if economic factors are taken into account, the impact is greatest for blue-collar groups, depending on adequacy of pension plans. Several factors must be taken into account, however, in assessing the impact of loss of social role, particularly if one focuses on the work role. Rabbi Rubenstein has noted that the only group for whom loss of social role is not a great threat is the very wealthy and therefore the very powerful. Their continuing wealth serves to maintain the position of patriarch, matriarch, sage, or senior partner. The professional person often falls into this same category, for even though one no longer practices medicine, teaching, ministry, or law, one still tends to be regarded as "Doctor," "Professor," "Pastor," or "Judge."

Loss of identity

Studs Terkel's book *Working,* based on extensive personal interviews, demonstrates that almost all Americans endow their work with profound philosophical, religious, ethical, and vocational values. Our work enables us to feel a part of the total scheme of things. It is the avenue by which we express not only our stewardship of life and energy, but our convictions and our values. And for most of us, work becomes an important part of the total personality structure; to a great extent, we are what we do. Notice how we introduce each other and ourselves; it is almost always by our work. This is particularly true of men, but is now becoming increasingly true of women. "This is Doctor Olson. He is an internist." "This is Mrs. Green. She has three children" (by implication her work is that of mother and homemaker). "This is Miss Klein. She was a teacher at Franklin Junior High School for many years." We find our place in society and define ourselves as persons much more by our work than by other criteria. In times past, particularly for the age cohort that now includes the "frail elderly," one's social role tended to be defined much more by family structures. "This is John. He's the son of Judge Carter." "She belongs to the Smith family, who live north of town."

Often the introduction of a retired person is awkward. There are no ready "handles" by which that person can be defined. It is often at this moment that the elder once more gets the feeling of being a "nonperson." Usually, of course, preretirement roles are relied on to help define the person, but what this says once again is that we are not just who we are; we are defined by our work.

One's work plays a significant role in the personality structure. In a culture with a marketplace orientation such as ours, work is not only the definer of the self, but the measure of one's worth. Employment counselors advise young people or those displaced by economic recession to "package yourself" or "sell yourself." This phenomenon poses a crucial problem for elders who are no longer "productively" working. The central issue can be put this way: "Am I still a worthwhile person, or am I worthwhile only insofar as I can do a full-time job or be productive in some way or other? Can I be worthwhile in different roles of life or because of the kind of person I am?" This question should be of special import to pastors in their ministry with elders. (We will return to the theological implications of this later.)

For many of us, work also has important psychological functions. It contains anxiety and offers an area for reality testing. Like the pioneer clearing in a primeval forest, our work provides ritual structures, avenues for activity, and encounters with reality that hold back the encroaching forest of worries and anxieties that otherwise plague us, particularly when we can't get to sleep at night. How often I have heard evidence of this in the hospital where active people are immobilized and comment, "You sure have a lot of time to think, lying here." In the confrontation between the responsibilities and tasks of our work and our fantasies about our abilities, dreams, and wishes, reality is revealed. Out of this confrontation a more realistic self-assessment of abilities and possibilities emerges, and we can more accurately deal with the responsibilities of mature living. When this arena of confrontation is no longer present, it is easy for dreams and fantasies or regrets and fears to take over. For this reason it is often important for psychic and spiritual health for the elder to have something to do, not just to satisfy our culture's heresy that we are only what we produce, but to enable us to maintain contact with a real world.

The role transitions called for in aging—retirement, developing a postretirement life-style, moving from one's home to condominium and later to retirement facility, and facing illness and death of oneself or spouse—are all closely related to the value hierarchy the person has developed. Gould has rightly observed that "we must do work that confirms our talents and expresses a psychodynamic theme close to the core of us."[3] If that central theme or value is the display of power and authority, or material gain and prosperity, then profound value shifts must be undertaken when work is laid aside. If, on the other hand, service to others, or the development of personal characteristics such as integrity, honesty, and love are the core, value shifts are not so profound. Indeed, such values can continue to be expressed also through one's so-called leisure years.

The effect of retirement on this value hierarchy, and the changes that may be required, offer the pastor an opportunity to assist the elder in a reexamination of the values that were being expressed by work. Explored, too, should be the manner in which these or more appropriate values can be expressed in the continuing life of elderhood. It may well be that the examination of the values being expressed through one's work should be a personal and pastoral agenda for the first round of individuation during the mid-life transition. For this reason the theological issues of vocation become a particular spiritual agenda for the "young old."

Loss of power

Also involved in the loss of work is the loss of power and authority. For most of us, work is the primary avenue through which power and authority are expressed. If they cannot be expressed in work, then various substitutions take place, such as the expression of power and authority in the home, in the church, in the social club or friendship circle. With retirement comes a loss of power and a loss of the avenues through which power can be expressed. A retired teacher, for example, no longer can expect others to read a book or write a report on it. A retired shop steward no longer has any authority over workmates. The conflict in aging here seems to be between a total loss of power or the possibility of a transmutation of power. In some cultures this is far less difficult than here in America; cross-cultural studies and experience have demonstrated that in most Third World cultures, older people generally experience more respect and dignity (a form of power) than in ours. Elders assume the role of sages; they are often still the governors of society, informally or through formal office holding. We see vestiges of this in congregational life, where elders are often a significant part of the informal power structure of the congregation, though they hold no office. When they lose even this power in the church, there is a bitterness toward "how the church has changed" and against the pastor. Pastors need to understand this loss of power so they can truly care for these older members, even when they become critical of the pastor for being an agent of their loss of power.

One of the reasons why elders are no longer so venerated in our culture has to do with technology. In an industrial assembly line economy, capability and safety issues require that elders no longer be actively involved in work. Rapidly developing scientific and information technology have also brought about a role reversal in teaching. In more primitive or agrarian cultures, it was the old who passed on the tradition of the clan. This is now no longer as necessary or possible. Books and other forms of communication can pass on the tradition, though they cannot communicate the life-style or manner of following the tradition. The media—radio, and particularly television—also are the carriers of the cultural tradition, thus rendering the elder sage obsolete. But not only are elders no longer needed as the carriers of tradition, they are no longer in as much demand as teachers of vocational or professional skills. This is illustrated by the new math phenomenon of a few years ago; suddenly parents could no longer help their children with homework. In some instances children had to teach the parents the new math. And now we see the same phenomenon with computers; fourth graders teach their parents how to use the computer.

Economic loss

A further loss associated with the loss of work is economic. Loss of work and regular income from work brings about a change in income, which for some may be profound, for others not so critical. Fortunately, most industrial societies have worked out pension systems to provide for the aged, but the increasingly dire prospect of continuing inflation (however modest) threatens to erode these once-adequate pension schemes. Though Simon de Beauvoir paints too grim a picture, it is a vision that should be kept in mind:

> Society inflicts so wretched a standard of living upon the vast majority of old people that it is almost tautological to say "old and poor"; again most exceedingly poor people are old. Leisure does not open new possibilities for the retired man; just when he is at last free from compulsion and restraint, the means of making use of his liberty are taken from him. He is condemned to stagnate in boredom and loneliness, a mere throw-out. The fact that for the last fifteen or twenty years of his life a man should be no more than a reject, a piece of scrap, reveals the failure of our civilization.[4]

We may again be entering an era where to be old is to be poor. This, at least, is the threat hanging over the heads of most people over middle-age, who have no more time to rebuild retirement plans to counteract continuing inflation.

Loss of safety

A related loss for elders is the loss of a sense of social safety, the fear of violence or a criminal attack. Every metropolitan newspaper carries the horror stories almost every day. Thieves know the day when Social Security checks are mailed out, and they lie in wait for the elderly victim. So widespread is the concern of elders for their safety and so pervasive is its effect, that many churches, at least in major cities, can no longer plan evening meetings. Perhaps the failure of our civilization is to be measured most by our failure to provide reasonable safety for vulnerable elders.

Loss of independence

The losses and the gains of aging are all a part of an interpenetrating whole, one loss related to and affecting another, one gain enhancing another or cancelling out a particular loss. Work loss is followed by a certain degree of economic loss, which in turn generates a loss of independence. The former freedom of two cars has to be given up for economy's sake, and the couple learns to make do with one car. Ultimately even that one car can no longer be driven when physiological-sensory losses take their toll and make safety a prime consideration. I know that one of the structures of independence that will be most difficult for me to accept will be the loss of ability to drive my car. This will be more than just the loss of the use of machine; a part of my "free spirit" will be sacrificed too.

In our culture, development or maturation requires that we move from an original state of great dependency in childhood to one of independence, if not self-sufficiency, in adulthood. The ideal of the self-made man or woman is strong in our culture. The ideal of maturity requires self-sufficiency, competency in managing one's own affairs, and a dislike of being a burden on others. These are attitudes, incidently, that militate against most of the biblical, ethical injunctions about relationships with fellow human beings. Loss of independence, in a way, means also loss of personal power and authority and dignity, so that gradually the elder begins to feel a victim of life, rather than a steward of life. Given the realities of our society and of aging, there may be little that can be done to counteract this loss, except to be sensitive to it and endeavor to minimize the various aspects of dependency and maximize personal capacity and power. A helpful rule of thumb is, "Do *only* for the elder what he or she *cannot* do for herself." Sometimes our willingness to be helpful, kind, and loving must be disciplined in this way.

Loss of time

After retirement there is both a gain and a loss of time. The future does not stretch out endlessly as for the youth; it rather stretches into eternity. But the present is filled with time; elders have "all the time in the world" upon retirement, but it is unstructured time. There is no clock to punch that provides discipline for getting all the things done that clamor for attention: the papers to file, the drawer full of material to be sewn into clothing, the slides to sort, the house to be done over, the relationships to be strengthened. Small wonder that many retirees complain, "I'm busier than I was when I was working full-time!" Successful retirees seem to be those who establish for themselves a regimen of time, a schedule that continues the useful habits of occupational life.

Spiritual losses

Those who are spiritually concerned for the elderly should take special note of the impact on the spirit of this manifold complex of losses. We have already noted the loss of personal dignity that frequently accompanies loss of productive work and loss of independence. It is easy for the elder to feel that she is only a "thing" to be discarded when no longer useful, rather than a person created in the very image of God, a fact that no amount of productivity or nonproductivity can change. Paul Pruyser has said, "The aged are subject to many indignities that are experienced as a frontal attack on their self-concept, their feeling of self-worth and the maintenance of mechanisms of self-regard."[5] Examples of the loss of personal dignity include the belittling of elders' opinions in decision making, a particular "sin" of professionals who work with older people. The role reversal that takes place in the family as aging parents gradually come to be treated as the dependent children of their own children, the various indignities of illness, and the increasing loss of personal privacy are other examples.

Linked to the erosion of self-esteem attending the physical-psychological losses in aging is the loss of a sense of dignity. For most elders the idea of "self-esteem" is expressed in the need for a sense of dignity, for being respected as a person. One's bodily and personal integrity, or privacy, is closely related to this. The loss of personal dignity is frequently expressed by society and experienced by the elder in the form of "infantilization." One of the myths of aging is that as people grow older they regress into a second childhood, and society is all too willing to help this process along. It may be that our culture cannot manage caring for others, those who are dependent, except by seeing them as children. To be a child is to be dependent; therefore, to be dependent, as older people must, is to become childish. I realized that I was joining the ranks of senior citizens one day when a waitress called me "Dearie." I have often been distressed to observe how many people, sometimes including staff in hospitals or skilled-nursing facilities, almost unconsciously fall into the pattern of treating residents and elderly patients as though they were small children. Almost as belittling to the elder's sense of dignity and self-esteem is the experience of condescension from younger folk.

Another form in which the loss of dignity occurs is when elders are stripped of the right to make their own decisions for their lives. One of the valuable insights of existentialism is the assertion "To live is to decide." Thus, not to be able to decide is almost nonliving. To be responsible under God and to other humans is a significant aspect of being created in the image of God. To deny persons this heritage is to depersonalize them, to strip them of the last vestige of self-esteem or personal dignity.

The impact of losses

As losses are faced with realism, courage, grief, and hope, they can not necessarily be conquered or overcome—but they can be assimilated. One can learn to live with them, and if need be, to die with them. The pastoral theologian will quickly recognize here the relevance of a "theology of the cross," which contends that life in faith under God is not one of continual conquests and victory (a "theology of glory"). Life here on earth, among creatures limited and self-limiting, caught in our common heritage of self-concern, frequently includes defeat, suffering, and pain. But defeat, suffering, and pain need not destroy us; nor are they evidence that God has deserted us or that our faith is so weak or our sin so great that we are getting what we deserve. A theology of the cross holds that through the tragedies and traumas of life God's compassion and love, and ultimately his life-giving power, sustain us. Our losses will always be losses, not necessarily alchemized into gains by some miraculous intervention.

Grief and bereavement will necessarily be a part of the aging process. The life of aging is filled with a thousand "little deaths": the death of the ability to play tennis with the same vigor as last year, the loss of one's wind after the second flight of stairs, the loss of ability to thread a needle without assistance, the loss of vision without glasses, the death of immediate erotic response, the loss of ability to touch the floor with one's fingertips, or of being able to squat and get up off the floor without major physical effort, the death, one by one, of high school classmates, good friends, colleagues, parents. All these continuous little deaths can make aging a time of almost chronic grieving if there is no help for the griever. Because the deaths do not come with dramatic impact, but overlap one another, the neat schedules of the grief process outlined by people like Kübler-Ross and others are not always relevant. One can be at the acceptance stage in grieving over lost youthful energy and at the denial stage of grieving over inability to manage one's fingers as dexterously over the handwork, the piano, the typewriter, or the musical instrument. But the sensitive pastor or friend knows that a listening ear and the refusal to order the sorrowing to "look at the bright side" or "cheer up" can be useful in guiding the person through the long valley of sorrows that growing old can be.

Looking at the gains

In spite of this rather formidable list of losses that are often a part of aging, there are gains in growing older. While attending a preretirement seminar, I was with a group of recently retired persons, and I was amazed and encouraged by the almost unanimous joy and happiness they expressed at being retired. They were looking forward with enthusiasm to growing older. There is something positive and ennervating to say about growing older! The poet Longfellow put it well:

> *What then? Shall we sit idly down and say*
> *The night hath come; it is no longer day?*
> *The night hath not yet come; we are not quite*
> *Cut off from labor by the failing light;*
> *Something remains for us to do or dare;*
> *Even the oldest tree some fruit may bear,*

. . . .

For age is opportunity no less
Than youth itself, though in another dress.
And as the evening twilight fades away
The sky is filled with stars, invisible by day.

Many of the final years of life can indeed be, and are for many, "golden years" to be enjoyed, with new and rich experiences to be shared. It is important for all of us, as we face our own aging, to be able to keep a balanced view between the losses and gains of aging, so that the losses do not color our expectations of aging so negatively that we fail to appreciate the real gains. This is particularly important for those who walk alongside elders in a helping role.

So we consider the gains of aging—physical-psychological gains, social gains, and emotional-spiritual gains.

Physical-psychological gains

The various areas of degenerative loss that we have earlier noted do, however, bring with them a certain gain. As one's capacities diminish, so do the vigorous drives to be active and busy. Lowered levels of energy allow one to take life a bit easier. The narrowed spectrum of vision and audition permit one to concentrate on aspects of life and experience that can be more meaningful. These same factors also aid one in refurbishing one's value hierarchy and centering life on values that do not depend so heavily on the material aspects of life.

With aging there seems also to be relative freedom from hormonal drives that propel us in sexuality and aggressiveness. In his book *On Aggression,* extrapolating from research and observation of lower life forms, Konrad Lorenz asserts that aggression is a normal attribute of human beings. Recent research has identified testosterone as the hormone most directly connected with sexual excitation in both male and female, and with aggressiveness in all primates. The normal decline of this hormone in aging is generally discernible in the middle years of life. In our later years when we are no longer so anxiety-ridden over the change in sexual drives and desires, we may be able to be both reflective and at peace with the reality that our engines are not "revving up" so fast. There is no longer either the drive, or the need, to make every relationship a conquest of either sexuality or power. In aging we can relax from needing to prove ourselves by winning every time. As poet May Sarton muses, "It is time to lay ambition and the world aside."[6]

Along with this comes a newfound sense of equanimity; it is not necessary for me to be number one in order to contribute meaningfully, to be myself. Dr. Lee Griffin has suggested that with this newfound sense of equanimity "I may find it possible that, though in small and perhaps only personally significant ways, the world around me is richer for my having walked here. With the removal of pressure to produce and excel, there is now emotional space and time to sniff the flowers."[7]

The process of "creative remembering" suggests further gains in aging as the psychological process of the memory changes with age. The larger picture of life can emerge when the memory is no longer preoccupied with details but excels in the reflective process. One can strive for the deeper meanings and the lasting values in friends, the beauties of nature, and the blessings of God.

In the psychological domain there is the relaxing of the defense mechanisms, as in aging we become less defensive and self-protective, caring increasingly less about "what people will think." In early life and into middle age, the human mechanisms by which we defend ourselves against the various forms of anxiety frequently distance us protectively from fellow human beings. With the relaxation of these defenses, there is not only more freedom to be ourselves, but also more freedom to enter into wholesome new interpersonal relationships.

Gains in the social domain

Are there any social gains when the older person faces the loss of the all-important work role? Robert Atchley, a social gerontologist, suggests an approach that may be useful in explaining adjustments to retirement. This is the continuity theory, which assumes that whenever possible the individual who has lost the all-important work role will cope with this loss by increasing time spent in roles that he or she still has, rather than attempting to find new roles to fill. The momentum of the structured routine of work continues especially into the first period of aging—the young old—but there is the gain of freedom from pressures to conform to time schedules and from the pressure to produce. There is now freedom to engage in especially meaningful aspects of the work role, as when the retired machinist engages in the hobby of building model railways, or the retired teacher engages in more detailed reading of subjects for which there was no time during a busy professional life. For such an individual the gain of pressure-free time is substantial. Often the result of this is a busier life than one had before retirement.

In this pressure-free atmosphere there is also time and energy to explore various "spin-offs" from the formal work or social roles one has held during occupational years. This freedom poses an opportunity for both the older person and the congregation or community-service institutions to explore alternative roles the elder may fill, to the mutual benefit of both. The theological issues of vocation come to new focus during this period.

Gains in relationships

Another gain in the social domain can be significant, particularly for those older people who do not fall into the "disengagement" pattern of aging. The poet May Sarton expressed it in this way: "There is another subtle change: we become contemporaries or nearly, of people who used to seem much older. Former teachers become friends; they, who seemed long ago when we were children to live on some Olympus light years away, are suddenly very close to us in actual age. We communicate at last as equals, and this is a new kind of delight." The sphere of our social relationships can expand as we grow older. I have found, corroborating Sarton's experience, that among my good friends are now those who were several classes ahead of me in school, almost 10 years older and inaccessible when I was 30. Now we are contemporaries. I have found, too, a different pattern of relationships with older relatives who were once looked up to but now are peers.

Our relationships with friends are also less demanding, more comfortable. Sarton said that friends in elderhood "old or new

. . . are seen in a different way now; loved less possessively, more for what they are, less for what we need from them."[8] This results from the relaxing of earlier defense mechanisms.

Gains in self-esteem

An altered and strengthened self-esteem is possible as one is freed from the cultural and economic necessity to define one's self in terms of what one *does* and is now able to be more and more what one *is*. This is expressed, for example, in the freedom now to do what one really *likes* to do instead of what one *should* do or *has to* do. One can pursue with some abandon the avenues of special interests, even pursue a postretirement career to fulfill some dream or sense of destiny that had to be buried beneath the responsibilities of productivity. There are notable instances of people who have started a whole new life after 65, like Grandma Moses or Winston Churchill. No longer is there the need to be dependent on what others think, because older people are expected to be individualists or even eccentric! One can even share personal credos and viewpoints with greater abandon, revealing one's innermost thoughts more freely and with more candor.

Gaining freedom

Growing out of this is the enhanced opportunity to become involved in social reform when elders make use of the freedom to share personal viewpoints with candor and abandon. Could it not be that elders are particularly open to the Spirit of the Lord, even as the prophet Joel portrays it?

> And it shall come to pass afterward, that I will pour out my spirit on all flesh; your sons and your daughters shall prophesy, your old men shall dream dreams, and your young men shall see visions (Joel 2:28).

Advocacy groups comprised largely of elders, like Grey Panthers, may indeed be an important avenue in our culture for the particular gifts of elders (reflecting intelligence, the wisdom of experience, the freedom from pressures of social conformity) to be exercised for the good of the nation itself, through active involvement in wise social reform.

The ability to rise above the limitations of aging and become involved in concerns seems to be one of the key factors in creative aging. M. L. Tobin demonstrated this by her involvement in social issues:

> People could be doing in their final years things they never had a chance to do before. All kinds of new things. I am trying to grow in love, friendship, an effort to do something about the perilous situation that we find ourselves in as a world, the whole nuclear threat. If I believe that human life is good, then I have to affirm that.[9]

Older people have more freedom and possibility to become involved in issues that are highly sensitive and controversial, but as Anne Bennet, who was active in the founding of Grey Panthers, remarked, "We are no hostages to fortune. We don't have any jobs to be fired from."

Aging can also bring tremendous gain to those who would learn firm and wholesome human dependencies. Fortunate is the older person, dependent on others in one way or another, who can experience that dependence as a blessing rather than to see it as a burden! Surely in the reflective years of aging we can discover the vacuity of the creed of self-sufficiency and begin to appreciate the joys of appropriate dependency, which is neither demeaning nor infantilizing. As one makes this discovery, dependence on the steadfast love and grace of God no longer seems so foreign or so difficult. This may be one reason why, for some elders at least, spiritual life gains more depth and meaning.

As one relinquishes the frenetic activity of the treadmill of work-a-day life, one may discover the possibility of venturing in depth where in the productive years one barely had time for a fleeting glance. Out of this must naturally grow another gain, a newfound sense of equanimity. It is no longer necessary for me to be number one in order to contribute meaningfully. I can accept the possibility that I am lovable just because I am me. As my engulfing propensity to be oriented upward and ever onward ceases, the here and now can come into clearer focus. Elders tend much more to be better able to live each day as it comes, with discernment and appreciation. There is time now to uncover deeper personal values and discern where these values may differ from those for which one has been working and from the culture in which one lives. This venture into deeper self-discovery can, and frequently does, provide the occasion for a deeper integration of the spirit. As one oldster succinctly put it, "I've got no boot to lick and nothing to lose. I might as well be me and enjoy it."

Open to perceive God

This more profound integration of the personality and reflection on the meaning of life and death uncovers another, somewhat paradoxical, gain, which occurs when one has finally come to terms with death. As my colleague Lee Griffin has reflected, "With the diminishing of external expectations and the escalating awareness that I, too, must cross the River Styx, I may well be afforded a fresh opportunity to discern the knocking on the door of my soul and to open it afresh to the promises of God."[10] What has been a more or less abstract reality, one's own dying, now becomes a more profound realization. "I am somewhat able to view the totality of life with its weaknesses and its strengths, its failures and its successes, its sorrows and its joys, its spring and summer and now autumn and winter."[11]

Freedom from shackles of death

When one has made one's peace with death so that it is no longer feared or denied, one finds a new freedom and zest for living. This sense of liberation from the shackles of death is not strange to the Christian who places full confidence in Christ's resurrection and looks forward in hope to the fulfillment of living that is our heritage beyond death. It is the exultation of Paul, "O death, where is thy victory? O death, where is thy sting?" (1 Cor. 15:55). But the aging person lives in this hope at a different level from the younger Christian, who rejoices in the Easter message as a reality far down the corridors of life's pilgrimage. The elder engages death, reflects on what it will be like to die, sees in the diminishments of aging the invitation to dialog with death, much as an aging Episcopal priest, Father Congrove, viewed it: "God is making all things dark and silent around me. . . . I must begin to long for home." Or as the aging Johann Sebastian Bach reflected in music, "Come, Sweet Death." One elder man eloquently commented, "There are some joys to old age, but none greater than realizing that finally you are learning about the important things. Perhaps God reveals some of his mysteries to us at the very end, before He receives us."[12]

Liberated from the terror of their own dying, the aged, particularly the frail elderly, are free to serve others better. Now in an ultimate sense, they have nothing to lose and everything to gain. These are the "old ones," the sages who can teach us all the art of holy living and holy dying. They are the ones who surprise seminary students who go to minister to them and discover instead that they have been ministered to. Every pastor has such elderly saints in the congregation who renew the joy of ministry by their gift. They are truly the wounded healers who have made peace with life's last great enemy, death, and are now free to share their peace. An 80-year-old woman planned a trip to Palestine. Her children were appalled. "Mother, you're too old and frail for a trip like that! What if you got sick over there?" She replied, "Well, I can't think of a better place to die than on the shores of the Sea of Galilee."

In summary, let us be reminded that aging is a process of coming to terms with both gains and losses. The gains of aging do not necessarily cancel out the losses and guarantee "golden years," nor need the losses inevitably sour the closing years of life. One comes to terms with both gains and losses, appreciating the gains and struggling with the losses, each in his or her individual style. Some are more adaptable and can deal with the losses in a way that does not cripple the spirit, while others rejoice in the gains almost to denying the diminishment of aging. A vital balance can be struck to incorporate both gains and losses in a way that makes life possible, even enriched. Often it is the pastor's opportunity to enter into the struggle and aid the elder in assimilating losses and gains, to help make continued living, and finally dying, a celebration of victory.

5

You Can Teach
an Old Dog

The adage "you can't teach an old dog new tricks" has become a self-fulfilling prophecy for many older persons (and for many an educational planner in the parish or the nursing home). It has inhibited or even blocked much of the intellectual and spiritual growth that could have taken place. Mounting evidence from neurological studies and other investigations into changes in intellectual processes accompanying old age now clearly shows that one does not lose one's mental powers with age; they only change, and may even be enhanced with age.

Recent discoveries

Investigations into the plasticity of the central nervous system (CNS) are providing one of the most promising foundations for continued creativity and development in the psychological-neurological domain of aging. While the number of neurons in the central nervous system decreases during the lifetime of the individual, through continual processes of adaptation and plasticity these neurons respond to stimulation and functional demands by sprouting new terminals, "thereby increasing the number of synaptic endings at any given neural junction and/or by changing the size and complexity of dendritic interconnections."[1] These authors note that the opposite effect can also result from sensory-deprivation injury to brain tissue. Is it possible that since we have assumed universal decline in aging, we have therefore neglected to stimulate older people, to engage them in the normal functions of life, and by putting them on the shelf have caused a deterioration that should not have occurred? The authors conclude, "The individual who chooses to perform activities which are meaningful to him and which are rich in a variety of sensorimotor experiences will promote neuronal complexity within his own nervous system. Ultimately his aging process is enriched and expanded because of the existence of an increased number of adaptive responses with which the stresses of aging can be met."[2] Elders who have remained vital and creative after the age of 80 certainly seem to demonstrate the truth of these findings.

The evidence from the study of intelligence supports this view as well. Though scores on the classic intelligence tests go down the older one gets, there is a question as to just what is being measured; often it is simply speed of response or even specific culture-related terminology. In a study reported in 1974, four generally independent dimensions of intelligence were found: (1) *crystallized intelligence,* including the skills one acquires through education and experience; (2) *cognitive flexibility,* which measures the ability to shift from one way of thinking to another, as when one must supply either a synonym or antonym to a word; (3) *visual motor flexibility,* involving shifting from familiar to unfamiliar patterns in tasks requiring coordination; and (4) *visualization,* the ability to organize and process visual materials.

Longitudinal studies have determined that there is no strong age-related change in *cognitive flexibility.* And for the most important dimension, *crystallized intelligence,* there was a systematic *increase* in scores for various age groups right into old age. People over 70 improved from the first testing to the second. This finding is confirmed by other studies that show that older adults *process* information more effectively. In studies in which random words are to be recalled, as compared to recall of meaningful phrases, youth were better at random recall, elders better at recall of meaningful phrases. While memory for exact detail declines, memory for logical relationships that call for abstractions, organization, and interpretation of learned material increases with age.[3] Provided we retain our health, have adequate stimulus from the environment in which we live, and continue to engage in learning and problem-solving tasks, our intellectual capacities will not diminish as we grow older.

A careful examination of recent research on aging has led Dr. Robert Butler, director of the National Institute on Aging, to conclude that scientific studies support the idea that learning capacities do not diminish with age. He concurs that intellectual abilities of healthy people grow through the years. The stereotypes of intellectual decline in aging are actually harmful, because they set up false expectations. If older people believe they cannot learn or remember, they will likely be anxious in learning situations and will withdraw from opportunities to learn. With intellectual functioning, as with many physical functions, the truth is, "If you don't use it, you lose it."

Elders are more likely than younger people to be blocked by factors such as fear of making a mistake or fear of appearing foolish. In 1968, a psychologist named Eisdorfer conducted research on age changes in learning and memory. He found that older people were doing substantially worse than younger people on just about every learning task. Acting on a hunch, he tested the different levels of physiological arousal between elders and youth and found that elders become more nervous in learning situations. After giving the elders a mild sedative that blocked autonomic nervous system arousal, performance differences between old and young learners were minimized. The autonomic nervous system has little to do with learning, but a great deal to do with our emotions. All of us know that we learn better when we are free from anxiety and worry. This is significant for the climate of parish learning for older adults.

Pete and Lillian, both in their 80s, had several years ago retired to a villa on the grounds of a church-related elderhome. After Pete died, Lillian's niece Joann visited and was pleased to see Lillian reading a large-print magazine with the aid of a magnifying glass. Lillian is blind in one eye and has only peripheral vision in the other. In the course of the visit, Lillian asked, reluctantly, "Pete is gone?" She had been afraid to ask the staff because she was embarrassed and anxious about sharing her confusion with them. Gently, Joann led Lillian's thoughts back through Pete's heart attack and death and helped her once more assimilate and understand what had happened.

One thing Joann avoided, however, was the way that Lillian had discovered that she was not to return to her home after the memorial service for Pete but was to be placed in the medical unit because she was an amputee in a wheelchair and could not care for herself. The decision (probably a wise one) was made by the administration and her closest relatives, but without consultation with Lillian. Joann was present when Lillian was told of the sudden move that was to be made. No amount of tears, dismay, ranting, or protest on Lillian's part could shake the decision that had been made for her.

Now, 18 months later, Lillian is still confused about Pete's death and her presence in this strange room that is supposed to be her home. She often thinks she is in a motel. As Joann reflected on her visit with Lillian, she said: "Is it any wonder that 18 months later she is still confused about Pete's death? I know she is physically well tended, but I question whether she has any stimulation to be the most that she can be. Lillian was by profession a businesswoman, a devoted, active Christian. Does anyone wheel her to chapel? To visit with other people? As much as I want the best for Lillian, how much more must God want for her?"

Here is a classic example of dealing with an elder based on the assumption that older people can no longer learn or understand; instead, they have to be managed by others, without being given opportunity or time to participate in the decisions about their own lives. This occurs frequently with the frail elderly, of whom Lillian is a good example. It is erroneously assumed that as the body becomes more frail, so does the mind. And if the mind is still functioning at all, it is assumed that the frail elder can certainly no longer learn and is in all probability "senile." Knowing that elders can always think and learn, that their minds will function until death, though in modified ways, can have profound implications both for how we treat them and how we continue to be involved in their growth through education.

The Swiss psychologist Piaget, who has studied learning in children and adults, has demonstrated that learning is an integrative activity. When integration takes place in learning, two things occur: the learner is modified, and the material learned is modified. The material being learned is modified by being integrated or included with what I already know, and as I integrate this new material, I am modified. Piaget called these two modes of modification "assimilation" and "accommodation." So in order for real learning to take place, I have to be willing to be changed, to accommodate myself to the new information that is available. Change can be difficult for all of us, so in order for a maximum learning situation to occur, change must pose a minimal threat.

The learning processes of assimilation and accommodation and the effect of the changes of aging suggest two important implications: (1) when we are young, we have a remarkable ability to carry around with us enormous amounts of relatively unintegrated information—trivia—much of which is often spontaneously integrated at a later time. Every serious college student has had many "aha!" experiences of spontaneously integrating information that earlier made little sense. At age 70, however, our capacity to carry around a great amount of trivia is less, but we are as likely as the youth of 20 to retain material that has been, or is, integrated; (2) since learning is an integrative process and since the capacity to spontaneously reorganize and integrate material that is not immediately meaningful decreases with age, it becomes important that activities that foster integration in learning take place. In providing education for elders in the church, we have to take special pains to create learning activities that are neither childishly meaningless nor boring. We should provide activities that promote immediate integration or assimilation and take care that accommodation (the threat of change for the person by learning) is minimized, so that the threat does not block learning.

To summarize this brief sketch of the research we note: (1) the adaptability of the central nervous system to respond to stimulation continues throughout life; (2) there is a systematic increase in what has been called "crystallized intelligence" as one grows older—the capacity to process information and draw conclusions from it; (3) there is a decline in the capacity to remember details; (4) older people tend to respond to learning situations with anxiety, which can block effective learning. The alleged difficulties elders have in learning and intellectual functioning, then, may be related more to motivation and situation than to degenerative deterioration.

Implications for adult education

In a class in which elders are mixed with youth, we can expect the elders to be reluctant to contribute, lest they make a mistake in details or appear foolish. A supportive atmosphere for learning is more important for older learners than for younger learners. Wrong insights should not be dealt with harshly in older learners. If the anxiety of "I'm afraid I'll make a mistake and make a fool of myself" can be reinterpreted to mean "I'm eager and anxious to learn about this, even though I might make a mistake," an elder—and for that matter a youth—can learn a great deal more and more easily. The context of learning is of crucial importance.

There are some additional implications of all this for parish programming. We know that the speed with which we process information diminishes slightly with age. That is not surprising, considering that there is the same slowdown in other bodily functions. Yet it is important to keep this in mind, however, in elder education. We should plan on covering less ground, get to the essentials, and strive to minimize extraneous detail.

We also know that the older we get, the more difficulty we have with divided attention. This means not only that we have more trouble doing two things at once, but we have more trouble moving from one subject to another and back again. This helps us understand why some elders have great difficulty in adjusting to hearing aids. An electronic hearing device picks up everything—all the crackling background noise, the scraping of chairs, coughing people, crying babies—distractions that the nervous system more or less automatically filters out in normal hearing. It is like a tape-recorded group conversation, with all the distractions and static that get picked up. Another implication of this matter of concentration is that most of our parish adult-education programs make use of discussion groups, which are aimed at personal integration of learning. But in a discussion group the participants wander all over the place, and it becomes hard to keep track of the subject. It may be helpful, then, in a discussion group with elders, that more control of the wandering subject be exercised by leaders, that issues be carefully identified and then taken up in serial fashion, and that leaders summarize more frequently than they might with a younger group.

Daniel L. Olson, who has supplied the data for much of this section, has integrated these findings into a particular style of education with elders, which he reports was developed by Professor Boomersheim of New York Theological Seminary.[4] In a Bible study session, after reading a passage of Scripture, the group is divided into twosomes. Each of the partners is instructed to tell the other the passage as if he or she were telling someone a story. Then the group looks at the passage again to see if anything has been left out in the telling. The group discusses the question, "Why did I leave that part of the story (or passage) out?" Next the story is role-played and the experiences of the role players are discussed. Finally, the participants look at the various characters of the story and consider, "Can I see myself in that character?" Some of these activities can be quite threatening to any group of people, particularly elders, but carried out in a supportive atmosphere, where people know each other quite well, they can stimulate integration and accommodation.

Spiritual growth in aging

It surely follows from the studies in age-related change that the moral-spiritual life would be markedly different from the bell-curve model. If, as one grows older, the capacity for crystallized intelligence—that is, abstracting meaning from information—increases, then surely our capacity for moral and spiritual development continues throughout life, given proper stimulation and motivation. And this is precisely the case. The philosopher Schopenhauer captured this in an interesting metaphor:

> Life could be compared to an embroidery of which we see the right side during the first half of life, but the back during the latter half. This back side is less scintillating but more instructive; it reveals the interpatterning of threads.[5]

As we grow older, we make our moral decisions less and less on the basis of logically derived principles and more and more on the recognition of the interconnectedness of self, society, and God's action. Relationships tend to become more important than principle. Aging becomes the schoolroom in which we can develop ever greater discernment of the "interpatterning of threads." Most cultures throughout the world have noted this and have therefore attributed greater wisdom and insight to the aging and the aged. Only in a technologically based culture is this not so true. Pastors can do much to stimulate this process of spiritual growth until the very end of life, especially through adult educational programs in congregations.

6

Faith Concerns of Elders

The pastor has a special responsibility to older persons, an opportunity to offer resources of perspective and meaning for growing older. The pastor is the steward of rich resources of revelation, tradition, and the experience of the people of God that can help provide that meaning. To do this requires a compassionate heart, a sensitive ear, and particularly the facility for theological reflection. We have given some attention to the heart and the ear. Now we want to focus on the art of theological reflection, an art which, in my judgment, is too often neglected by parish pastors and mistakenly thought to be the province only of the academic theologian.

Pastors have often relied on the rich and valuable resources of the behavioral sciences for understanding the processes of aging and developing the skills for listening to elders. So rich and valuable have these resources been that we have tended to neglect the heritage of our faith and its traditions, which also make a significant contribution to caring for and guiding elders through their pilgrimage. Elders long to see their experience through the eyes of faith.

Amalie is age 73, a widow with an adopted daughter who is now taking responsibility for her. She lives in a church-related nursing home. She is a lifelong member of a local church. She walks slowly but gets around quite well; she has a nervous "tic" and is slightly hard of hearing. After a conversation about her enjoyment of walking and about some of her health concerns, she goes on to say, "If only this eye wouldn't twitch so."

Visitor: You get anxious about your eye?

Amalie: I shouldn't complain. The Lord has been good to me. I've never been sick and I still have Marianne (her adopted daughter) and George (her brother).

Visitor: You think God has been good to you?

Amalie: He has been very good to me. I'll just put up with it now till my time comes.

Visitor: Do you think this is God's way?

Amalie: I think so. I'm not good for anything anymore.

Visitor: What makes you think you're not good for anything?

Amalie: What can I do? Nobody pays any attention to an old woman. Oh, everybody is nice to me, but there isn't anybody who listens to me like you do. How come you are so interested in me?

Visitor: I like you and want to share some of the things you think about, and be your friend.

Amalie: You'll think I'm silly too. You'll lose interest in me. Nobody wants to listen to an old lady.

Some visitors might have responded to Amalie's question, "Why are you so interested in me?" by saying something like "Well, because God is interested in you," or perhaps "Because Jesus wants me to care for you." But to do that would have depersonalized the caring that was going on. Those responses would have been the correct theological *words:* God indeed does care for Amalie; Jesus did die for her. But Amalie's experience, in spite of those theological phrases, is that she is lonely and does not sense God's caring in any personal relationship. Thus her experience, and the experience of countless other saints of the Lord who feel the same loneliness, speaks to theology. Theological words often are not enough to convey the message to Amalie's experience and situation. The visitor sensed this, and therefore did not respond with words alone.

On the other side of the dialog, there are a host of questions that Amalie's experience flings at the corpus of faith. They have to do with the doctrine of vocation ("I'm not good for anything anymore") and the doctrine of the providence of God ("I shouldn't complain. The Lord has been good to me"). Where is the doctrine of grace in all this? "What can an old woman do? Nobody pays attention to an old woman," Amalie comments, as if to say, "Does God stop paying attention to us when we can no longer be productive?" And then there is that most difficult question, "Well, just how does God express his caring for one who is no longer good for anything?" Or, for that matter, "How does God as Spirit care directly for anyone?" These are the questions that should preoccupy pastoral theologians as they visit with these elders. These are issues of particular concern to Amalie's pastor, along with speculation as to the origins of her tic, or the cause for the nervousness that this conveys, or the sociological aspects of her family and institutional staff support systems.

Pastors frequently fall into the same stereotyped agism as everyone else. We, too, may think, "One old person is just like another." This is evident in our pastoral theology and pastoral care. It is too easily assumed that all older people have pretty much the same spiritual or theological concerns—loneliness, dealing with pain, facing death. But this is far from reality. Each person over 65 has as unique a spiritual concern as does each individual of 37, or each child of 12. One can, in a general way, group the spiritual concerns of elders in much the same way as can be done with persons of other age groups. We know from study and pastoral experience that adolescents, for example, have different concerns than do children under 10. We know, too, that adolescents at age 13 have different concerns than do 17-year-olds. So it is with older persons.

I have earlier suggested that it is useful to think of persons over 65 in terms of three age-groupings—the *young old*, the *middle old*, and the *frail elderly*. I wish to take up the idea that each of these age cohorts has specific spiritual concerns that are dominant over others. While this generalization is not yet born out by empirical research, geriatric chaplains with whom I have shared it are in agreement.

Faith concerns of the young old

The issue of vocation and stewardship of life is one of the primary concerns of the *young old*. There are at least three special times in life when the matter of vocation is most pressing. "What shall I do with my life?" is a particularly burning question during adolescence and the entry into adulthood. It arises again during the middle years (the mid-life crisis) as one reassesses his or her sense of destiny. It arises once again at entry into elderhood, which in our culture occurs most frequently with retirement. As the older person relinquishes the full-time responsibilities of work and when one's income no longer depends on daily work, the issue reasserts itself, "What shall I do with the life that is left to me?" Actually this question should be asked in the years or months preparatory to retirement. It would not be at all amiss for the pastor to consider this question with people in their early 60s, as they contemplate retirement, for it *is* a theological question.

This process of retirement has been described by Dr. John Bennett, who, until his retirement, was the president of Union Theological Seminary and a prominent teacher of social ethics, as *disengagement* and *reengagement*. "Obviously, when you retire from your main job you don't hang around trying to make trouble for your successor," he says. "But I think *reengagement* is important as well." Reengagement can be a reentry into the warp and woof of creative responsibility, of continuing participation in God's creative activity in the world. Bennett goes on to say,

> Elderly people still have a good deal of vitality. I don't think that we should let them sing their last song. We shouldn't put people between sixty-five and eighty in the same category as people who are older than that. We should have great flexibility and think of people as individuals, and expect a lot more from them."[1]

Retirement need not become a time when you are just put up on the shelf. It is very clear to anyone who is willing to listen to people in this age cohort that there is a continuing need and desire to be useful, to be seen as making a continuing contribution to society, the economy, the community, the family, and the church. All too often in retirement it is only in the family structure that there is opportunity for such a continuing contribution.

Vocation

The root and ground of our vocation is Baptism. God's call to us to enter into his work of continuing creation in the world was issued to us in our Baptism, and it is baptismal faith that generates and empowers us to respond to that call. We are not called directly to the service of God, however, but to the service of our neighbor. "Man is free to live according to God's will, as a worker together with God in vocation, in the interest of service to the neighbor," observed Gustav Wingren in his study *Luther on Vocation.*[2] Like Baptism and its blessings, this call remains with us throughout our lifetime; there is no retirement from Christian vocation.

The arena in which vocation is enacted, according to Luther, is the place where we are. Luther said this to counter the medieval notion that one could best, or perhaps only, serve God by retreating from the world into some monastic hideaway. A modern counterpart of this is the notion that vocation has only to do with "church work." Wingren observed, "Since it is in my situation on earth that I meet my neighbor, my vocation comprehends all my relations with different neighbors; indeed my vocation can be said to consist of all those relations." This understanding originates from Paul's word to the Corinthians:

> Only let everyone lead the life which the Lord has assigned to him, and in which God has called him. . . . Every one should remain in the state in which he was called. Were you a slave when called? Never mind. But if you can gain your freedom, avail yourself of the opportunity. For he who was called in the Lord as a slave is a freedman of the Lord. Likewise he who was free when called is a slave of Christ (1 Cor. 7:17-22).

"There is no way to do God's will in a sinful world except as we meet the demands of our standing place," writes Martin Heinecken, now well into his retirement years.[3]

What this suggests for the Christian who ponders life after retirement and for the pastor who shepherds is that there is no retreat from the world. You are still called to be involved, according to the demands of your place in life, even though you have given up occupational or professional roles. You are still set in a network of human relationships as friend, wife or husband, father or mother, colleague or citizen. In those relationships with God-given neighbors, you can continue to be the channel of God's creative and redeeming love by your loving concern for your neighbor's well-being. Even after retirement, one still has resources of physical health, strength, capability or special talent, time and energy, and perhaps wealth with which to serve one's neighbor. How we perform that service will depend on the nature of those variables.

Consideration of talent, ability, and opportunity in finding one's postretirement vocation then, is as important as it was in the adolescent years. Too often elder vocations are not fulfilling because the elder is "underemployed." This is best illustrated by the congregation that utilizes the retired banker to take up the offering (because, presumably, this has something to do with finances). The vocation might be far better fulfilled if the banker were the treasurer of the congregation, or better yet, the financial and business advisor for all aspects of the business of the congregation. As one considers various volunteer opportunities with elders, not just any volunteer work should be sufficient. The challenge is not just to fill the retiree's time, but rather to meet needs with the talents and resources the retiree can provide. The vocational question is, "How can I respond to my neighbor's need where I am and with what I am."

Grace and Vocation

A second principle of a biblical doctrine of vocation is that our standing before God is not affected by the skill or success with which we discharge our vocation. This is always important, at whatever time of life, but it is of particular importance for the older person. One of the severe threats of retirement is the feeling of being worthless now that one is no longer economically or socially productive. This feeling has theological dimensions as well; many elders have felt the threat of abandonment by God once they could no longer be active, especially in church work. Anna, an elder who was being visited by a parish volunteer, expressed this concern:

Anna: Did the pastor send you out to see me?

Visitor: No, he didn't. I just wanted to keep in touch and see how you are getting on.

Anna: He's been out to see me, you know. I keep telling him that he needs somebody like me to talk with. Everybody needs a sounding board, you know, somebody to bounce ideas off of. And besides, I get a lot better feeling for what's happening in that church. People say things to me that he would never hear.

Visitor: What was the pastor's response to that?

Anna: He never really answered me. Did you ever notice how some people do that—they never answer your questions? Sometimes pastor never even says anything. Why, the last time I was in church, that was three months ago [she is recovering from a hip operation], he didn't say anything to me. I was feeling so down in the dumps, so depressed that . . . well. All it would have taken was just for him to have given me a cheery word, but he didn't even seem to notice me. Not even a touch did he give me. I'm not sure he even saw me, and nobody else seemed to either.

Visitor: You must have felt that no one cared about you.

Anna: Ain't that the truth? Why, I was wondering if God cared. Sometimes he just seems to let my troubles keep stacking up. They just keep coming one after the other, and they never seem to stop, even for a little while. It seems to me that once in a while God could give me a little time just to get even with them, but they just keep on coming.

It is difficult, especially in our culture, to overcome the idea that our importance to God depends on our usefulness. So the doctrines of grace and the promise of Baptism are the essential backdrop to the doctrine of vocation and have special meaning to elders. Thus it is important for pastors to be astute in teaching the doctrine of vocation.

How easy it is to try to engage the young elderly into one or another aspect of church work in such a way as to subtly undercut a grace-oriented doctrine of vocation. We frequently motivate people by guilt rather than by gratitude and a sense of stewardship, particularly when it comes to church work. We so easily make people feel that God will abandon them if they do not serve productively. Vocation, being called to serve, always requires the free response of a freely made decision to answer the call in accordance with one's place in life, one's opportunity, and one's talent.

One of the real blessings of a sense of vocation is that it provides meaning for life. This is obviously true for those who are still actively engaged before retirement. But can life have meaning without an occupational role? "How can I serve my neighbor now that I no longer have a clear social role, limited income, a weakened body, and decreasing strength?" may be the question that plagues the young elderly. It is at this point that a pastor can be helpful by guiding a careful assessment of strengths and liabilities and by identifying needs outside the network of one's primary social relationships.

Though the question of vocation comes to us in the first stage of elderhood, it does not leave us, but remains until death itself. Engraved on my memory is one of the last conversations my wife and I had with her mother, at that time 85, sitting in her room in a nursing home. Already her eyes had degenerated so that she could barely read on some days. And she, who had been a particularly intelligent and perceptive woman in earlier years, was plagued and embarrassed by the fact that it was sometimes impossible to remember the thought with which she had started a sentence. She felt she couldn't carry on a conversation, so the fabric of her relations with others was wearing very thin. In our conversation she kept asking both of us, "Why doesn't God take me? I'm just so useless here. There's nothing I can do anymore." How painful it was for her to recognize this, she who had done so much for so many all her life. "What's the purpose of my living now?" She pressed for an answer. Finally, my wife responded with, "Well, mother, you're the oldest one in our family, perhaps you can be an example for us on how to be old—and how to die." That is fulfilling one's vocation. She has done that.

Faith concerns of the middle elderly

Our youthful assumptions about aging would suggest that the question of death is put off until the very last minute, and therefore is the concern of the frail elderly, the final stage of life. For some it may well be, but chaplains of nursing homes, largely populated by the frail elderly, report that this question of dying and death, and for the Christian, hope of eternal life, is wrestled with earlier and is for many settled by the time they reach the age of 80 or so. This was the finding of Pastor Larry Trachte, who conducted a research project with 102 elderly residents of Iowa on *The Meaning of Aging*."[4] Trachte found that the frequency with which people thought about death was the highest in the age group of persons 71-75 (8%), second highest in the 86-90 age group (7%), and third highest in the age group 66-70 (6%).

The feelings about death varied, Trachte reports. Twenty-eight percent responded with predominantly negative feelings about death: fear, worry, or sadness. On the other hand, 36% responded with what might be regarded as positive feelings about death; 21% felt happy, and 13% felt relieved. Thirty-eight percent expressed ambivalent feelings toward death. "It makes me feel both sad and happy at the same time," was a typical response.

In this sample of religious persons the hope of life after death was predictably high. Eighty-seven individuals expressed feelings that life after death was "very important or important to them." Seven others felt it was "not very important." Trachte observed: "It is interesting to note that the importance of the hope for life after death actually decreases with the age of the respondents."

In response to the interviewer's question "If you had one wish, what would it be?" sample responses related to death included, "to end soon," "to die without pain," "to go to heaven," "to die while I'm asleep," "to meet my family in heaven," "early death," "that I could be loved by my family and die a painless death." One particularly interesting finding in the Trachte study is that nursing-home residents seem to think about death less than those who live in their own homes or live with family. Nursing-home residents were willing to talk about death in an almost matter-of-fact manner. It should be remembered in this connection that a much higher proportion of people over 80 are nursing-home residents.

Another finding of interest in the study is that those who are happiest in their present life are most likely to respond positively with regard to their feelings about death. "Twenty of the twenty-two persons who felt 'happy' about dying either felt 'very happy' or 'generally happy' about living," reported Trachte.

Facing the realities of death and dying is one of the most difficult tasks confronting human beings. Some, notably Ernest Becker, author of *The Denial of Death*, have contended that denying death is one of the driving forces of human motivation.[5] Viktor Frankl, the existential psychiatrist who experienced living death in the Holocaust, observed,

> What threatens man is his guilt in the past and his death in the future. Both are inescapable, both must be accepted. Thus man is confronted with the human condition in terms of fallibility and mortality. Properly understood, it is, however, precisely the acceptance of this twofold human finiteness which adds to life's worthwhileness, since only in the face of guilt does it make sense to improve, and only in the face of death is it meaningful to act.[6]

Indeed, as Christians, we see the very gospel as the call from death to life, and in Christ's resurrection our only hope of rescue from the sting of death.

Shepherding through Death

In one sense, the whole of our pastoral ministry is the shepherding of people out of death into the light and life of the gospel. Ours is the task of nurturing baptismal faith so that the dying person might through death continue in life eternal. The advice given to preachers can well also be given to the pastoral visitor: "Preach as a dying man (or woman) to dying men (or women)." As we age, each of us confronts death on several fronts, as it were; in the bereavement at the death of loved ones, loss of health, career, and in facing our own dying. Bereavement is the anticipatory echo of our own dying. What is needed as we work through these "little deaths," and face dying itself, is a faith for dying.

The ground of such faith can only be the grace of God. But for the elder this grace is not the abstract "unmerited favor" of theological definition but the living promise, "I am with you to the end of the age." It is the fulfilled longing of aging Anna that her pastor would pay attention to her, hear her, touch her. Grace for the elder is the "I will never!" to her prayer, "Thou, O Lord, art my hope, my trust, O Lord, from my youth. . . . Do not cast

me off in the time of old age" (Ps. 71:5,9). Grace is the unbreak-
able covenant God made that "neither death, nor life, nor angels,
nor principalities, nor things present, nor things to come, nor
powers, nor height, nor depth, nor anything else in all creation,
will be able to separate us from the love of God in Christ Jesus
our Lord" (Rom. 8:38-39). Grace is far more than the love and
acceptance of God, which we enjoy feeling. As fallible sin-scarred
people, we all know there is much in our life story that could
well destroy all love, perhaps even in family or friends. How then
can we trust in the image of love and affection, even in God,
given our human intellect's need to fashion God in our own
image in order to understand? God's durable covenant of grace
is his unconditional commitment to us. It is something an elder
can trust in. Grace is God's determination that nothing shall be
permitted to separate us from him.

Facing death

As we face dying and death, all of us wonder how we would
act in the agonizing pain of terminal illness. Will we lose our grip
on the childlike faith in God's love and mercy and feel more like
Job's wife wanting to "curse God and die"? What happens in the
long hours of coma, when faith, along with all sentience, seems
to be gone? What happens when, because of a stroke, no faith
response can be verbalized or even thought? Does the durable
covenant still hold then? There is a verse of the hymn "O Sacred
Head Now Wounded" that was the favorite prayer of my aging
father and mother. A free translation shows how the original
German text by Paul Gerhard expressed the real concern of the
dying person:

> *When I in time depart,*
> *depart thou not from me!*
> *When death I'm called to suffer,*
> *be thou near at hand.*
> *When in that hour I'm stricken*
> *with terror of the heart,*
> *deliver me from anguish,*
> *by power of your dying anguish.*

If we ask older people, or for that matter almost anyone, what it is about death that they fear most, we frequently find that it is not death, but dying. We fear the pain, the loss of self-discipline that occurs as we collapse in the face of pain and threat. When we are completely helpless, will we still be respected, cared for, loved? The grace of God does speak also to this, as Gerhard's beautiful hymn and the biblical account of the agonies of Jesus' crucifixion make clear. This is the durable promise that we shall not be bereft in the hour of our dying. "God shows his love for us in that while we were yet sinners, Christ died for us. Since, therefore, we are now justified by his blood, much more shall we be saved by him from the wrath of God" (Rom. 5:8-9).

But the elder whose grasp of faith is threatened by despair, suffering, and insentience and who is facing an increasing dearth of loving human relationships that might mirror the love of God, will wonder, Does this still apply to me? It is then that Paul's words are so meaningful:

> Do you not know that all of us who have been baptized into Christ Jesus were baptized into his death? We were buried therefore with him by baptism into death, so that as Christ was raised from the dead by the glory of the Father, we too might walk in newness of life. For if we have been united with him in a death like his, we shall certainly be united with him in a resurrection like his (Rom. 6:3-5).

Baptism, the individualized sign and seal that these promises apply to me, is the sacrament for the aged as much as for infants. United with Christ in Baptism, we can trust that dying no longer poses the threat of separation from God but is the gateway to resurrection.

In Trachte's study, the older person's hope in resurrection contained elements of longing for reunion with family and friends, release from suffering, simple rest, and finally the expectation of meeting the Savior. In these and similar statements, which every pastor who listens to elders has heard, we have the experiential content of eschatology. Elders are not concerned with proof of the resurrection or of the significance of resurrection for Christology; they embrace this gospel far more intimately with the question, "What will it be like for me?" A pastoral theology must address that, as does the apostle Paul in his letters (cf. 1 Cor. 15:35 ff.).

The New Testament doctrine of the resurrection of the body, therefore, is of primary concern to elders confronting dying. What does it promise? Will I have a body wracked with arthritis, a body minus several organs resulting from radical surgery? These are the kinds of questions many elders would like to discuss with their pastors but are afraid to ask (and pastors are perhaps grateful that they don't!). Hans Schwarz has suggested that understanding resurrection of the body in terms of a literal bio/physical revivication raises several problems and falls short of what Scripture means.[7] Joseph Sittler, in an interview at the time of his 75th birthday, commented: "I certainly do not want to continue to love the present carcass into all eternity. That is an absurd and not at all a pleasant idea."[8] And most elders would agree. South Sea islanders used to put their elders to a merciful death before they became infirm, in order to forestall what they thought would be a life in eternity with the crumbling old body in which they died.

When Scripture speaks of resurrection of the body, what is meant is the resurrection of the *person*. Always Scripture views human beings as embodied persons, but as to the shape of that body, Scripture is silent. Sittler further commented, "What life beyond death might be I have no notion. If all life is engendered and created by God, then that relationship will certainly not be destroyed. . . . Something continues, but what that will be, I'm perfectly willing to leave in the hands of the Originator."

In responding to the question, What can we look forward to when we hope and believe in the resurrection of the body? Hans Schwarz said that resurrection does not in any way involve the continuation of our present life, for resurrection is a "reality which involves the whole being" as can be inferred from the array of antitheses that Paul puts forth (1 Cor. 15:42-57).[9] Nothing is exempt from the new creation that will be. If we no longer live in dishonor, are no longer limited by the physical world, no longer age, are no longer distinguished by certain sexual relationships (Matt. 22:30), no longer face death, the I which we are and which died will be very different from the I which will be resurrected.

Yet we will be recognized as Christ was recognized by his disciples, though he was no longer bound either to time or space (John 20–21). Our identity in grace resides not in *who* we are but in *whose* we are. It is constituted by our relationships, by our loves (and in this life by our hates), by those who love us (and who hate us). So, related to Christ, and the community of fellow heirs of glory, our humanness undergoes profound changes along with our identity, which nevertheless remains constant in the fulfillment of baptismal grace.

So for the Christian, dying and the doorway of death are an entering into the sleep with the faithful. Luther often described this state as "deep sleep without dreams."

> Since death is called a sleep, we know that we shall not remain in it; but we shall awake and live again. . . . It will seem as if we had just dropped off, so that we shall rebuke ourselves for having been appalled and frightened at so fine a sleep in the hour of death.[10]

And with his delightful concreteness, Luther once noted, "We shall sleep until he comes and knocks at the tomb and says, 'Dr. Martin, get up!' Then in one moment, I will get up and I will rejoice with him in eternity."

In eternity—the fulfillment of time, rather than infinite time—Schwarz has pointed out, "all life-impairing defects of time will be overcome, transition, suffering, decay and death are all inextricably connected with temporality and change."[11] Eternity is living in God's eternal presence with the saints. In this hope we can learn the art of dying gracefully.

Facing living and dying in hope

The theologians who concern themselves with the Christian hope see this hope as having two dimensions or directions, both of which have importance for elders. Since there are not two English words for hope or for the future, they use two words from the Latin: *futurum* and *adventum*.

Futurum means the future that will be, which grows out of the past, the accumulation of all our past experiences and memories, the accumulation of our history. It is what we mean when we say, "In five years I will retire, God willing," as we consider the accumulation of our vocational years and see the summation of our calendar years. Involved in this future are the inevitable changes that the pilgrimage of aging brings upon us. The accumulating years can bring a bitter harvest, but they may also bring joy as we rest from our labors and reap the rewards of affection from family, especially grandchildren. This hope rests upon the consequences of our past pilgrimage, good or ill, extending themselves into the future. It may be described as the trajectory of our past into the days and years ahead. The spiritual dimension of this future is portrayed in the first letter of Peter:

> Blessed be the God and Father of our Lord Jesus Christ! By his great mercy we have been born anew to a living hope through the resurrection of Jesus Christ from the dead, and to an inheritance . . . kept in heaven for you, who by God's power are guarded through faith for a salvation ready to be revealed in the last time (1 Peter 1:3-4).

The Creator of an orderly universe has established the possibility of this future as an expression of structure and predictability in life. Elders understand and depend on order in planning their lives. We depend on the fact that savings laid aside in pension plans or Social Security will accumulate and be a dependable source of future income. When this is threatened, as in times of economic inflation, a serious threat faces elders. Also in human relations—as parents, or family members, or friends— we look forward to harvesting the accumulated concern and love and care of children in our own future. But the loss of friends and family, the "little deaths" along the pilgrimage, the hopes in the future turn into fear and loneliness. So we also anticipate continued reasonable good health as the accumulation of careful attention to diet, exercise, and the good stewardship of physical and emotional resources, and we dread the advance of disease. The principle that "whatever a man sows that he will also reap" (Gal. 6:7) is an expression of God's orderly universe. God is present in this future with both judgment and blessing.

But for elders it is vital that there be more to our hope for the future than simply the projected accumulations of the past. Liberating hope lies in our anticipation of the God who is the creator of "a new heaven and a new earth" coming down the path of life to meet us. The anticipations of Advent, the other form of hope, are not bound by the accumulations of the past, but transcend them. This advent hope does not arise out of the past, but is totally new. Coming to us not out of the past into the future, but from the future into the now, it offers a hope that transcends the accumulation of past mistakes, false turns, missed opportunities, lack of courage, and sin. This understanding of the future is nearer to the biblical understanding of "new creation." It is the affirmation of 1 John 3:2: "Beloved, . . . it does not yet appear what we shall be, but we know that when he appears we shall be like him."

We seem to be bound by what we have been becoming all our lives, but in the mercy of God we will surmount that and will be, instead, as Christ is. The kingdom parables of Jesus hint at the shape of this advent future with their surprise endings, which upset the old order or old way of looking at things.

There is both judgment and grace in this advent hope. For the dying, entry into the presence of God brings anticipated judgment as well as promise of mercy for those who stand before that judgment throne clad in the robes of the Lamb. But there is a particular blessing to elders in this advent hope. Human hopes rest only on the future—the trajectory of the accumulated past—since that is the only reality we human beings know. This is the only form of hope open to those who have not heard or have not accepted the good news. But the advent hope is God's creative breaking into, and breaking apart of, the accumulations of our history with the promise of the radical new life in resurrection, which is beyond our comprehensions or imagination. This advent hope says that God is not bound by human history, nor our individual accumulated past, but in powerful mercy transcends it. Our hope is for a new being which does not depend on our decisions, but solely on the gracious promise of a loving Father. In this hope we can as pastors guide elders in the *ars moriendi,* the art of holy dying.

It seems certain that in pastoral care we will have increased opportunities and expectation to be shepherds "through the valley of the shadow of death." The continuing elongation of the period of elderhood, the technological and ethical dilemmas of the care of the dying, and the increase of the hospice movement with its special opportunity to deliberately guide people through ˙ death will require us pastors to give more attention to this aspect of the care of our elders.

7

Faith Concerns of the Frail Elderly

Sometimes I can't understand why God has not taken me. I keep going in and out of the hospital. I know that my heart will not get any better. My daughter and her family have to do almost everything for me. I just sit in my chair and watch the days go by. I can't read anymore. My eyes are bad. Sometimes I wonder why God waits so long to take me. It's so hard to understand why I have to keep on suffering. I keep praying for God to take me. I've suffered many years, and there is no reason for me to stay on this earth. I've had a good life. If only God would take me.

Mrs. Raum, a 79-year-old widow and a lifelong member of the church, voiced the concerns that seem uppermost for the frail elderly: the meaning of suffering and the providence of God. These are not the exclusive concerns of people in the last stage of life. They may arise at any time, but they do come into sharper focus in the closing months of life.

Suffering

Dorothy Soelle, a German theologian, in her book *Suffering*, has looked deeply into human suffering through her experiences with war refugees (Fortress, 1975).[1] She has noted three phases of suffering: (1) mute suffering, (2) the anguished cry of lament, and (3) liberation for change. In mute suffering all one's physical and emotional energy is consumed in fighting the pain. This generates the isolating character of severe pain, which, when suffered in silence, creates even greater isolation. It is as if a sufferer does not want to drag another person into the mire of pain in which he or she struggles. So the elder often tries to shrug off compassion or sympathy with, "Don't bother about me, I can take care of myself," or remains in isolation out of the inordinate fear of being a burden. As the person continues in this mute struggle, there are three options: to become outwardly indifferent and hardened to pain, to just keep it to one's self, or finally, to begin reaching out and dealing with suffering in some creative fashion.

The antidote to this chasm of isolation is not indifference, nor a command to ourselves to become more sympathetic. Rather it is the internal integrity and strength that allows a pastor to enter another's suffering and loneliness without feeling either threatened or repulsed. But entering into another's suffering must be done in such a way so as not to further deteriorate the sense of worth and integrity of the suffering person. The motivation to reach out and work on the suffering must come from outside the sufferer. Someone must reach down into the well of loneliness. This is the ministry of pastoral initiative.

The anguished cry of lament, the second stage of struggling with suffering, is the cry of the psalmist: "Out of the depths I cry to thee, O Lord! Lord, hear my voice!" (Psalm 130). For those who have suffered in silence, it is only the intensity of their anguish that finally wrings this cry from their lips. It is not easily heard. We who hear it too often respond with admonition: "Don't be such a complainer." Simone Weil said, "Everyone despises the afflicted, though practically no one is conscious of it." It so nearly confirms the stereotype we have of the frail elderly: "They are such complainers." Perhaps they need to complain chronically, to make us hear their lament.

Very often this lament carries with it an anguished question, "What have I done to deserve this?" (meaning "Why is God punishing me so?"). For the elder who has little left in life but accumulated memories and now has little to look forward to but continuing suffering and loneliness, life seems to hold nothing but the unremitting punishment of God. In those dark hours even the most honorable and upright elders can remember "the sins of youth" and wonder whether they might deserve their suffering. These bitter herbs of memory can wipe out any perception of a gracious and merciful God. All too easily the extent of suffering and pain can become the measure of God's disfavor.

It is important that we hear the cry of lament not only as a cry of pain and a complaint against the seemingly hidden God. It may be both of these, but it is also a cry for help, an effort to reach out for a personal connection with someone outside the burning ring of suffering. How relieving it is for the sufferer to put into words the pain, the wondering, and the anger which suffering generates. And to have these words also come from a psalmist is powerful evidence that God is not repulsed by our anguished cries.

Pastoral response to this outcry can become a bridge of compassion. Once the bridge of compassion has been established, the process of "codetermination," as Soelle called it, can take place. Both sufferer and compassionate friend consider the meaning and function that suffering might have. This is what was taking place between Emma F. and her pastor:

Pastor: You sense a conflict within yourself between a faith that wants to believe in God's love for you and doubt whether God is really as active in delivering you as he could be?

Emma: Yes, that's how I feel, and I don't know if I should really be feeling that way at all. Do you suppose God could be working through me even as I am expressing these doubts that things don't somehow add up?

Here the sufferer is trying, with the help of another, to see how suffering might be used. This is to see suffering as "labor pains," as Soelle put it, giving birth to a larger reality of meaning and relationship.

Out of this collaborative work emerges the stage of liberation for change. As communication continues, the pain and anguish of suffering is shared, along with the doubts and fears. The suffering elder begins to be liberated from the island of bitter loneliness into the experience of shared anguish. Through this, strength is also shared for dealing with suffering as well as probing its meaning. So the pastoral task with those who suffer may become exploring how the suffering can be used to produce character and finally hope, as Paul suggested:

> We rejoice in our hope of sharing the glory of God. More than that, we rejoice in our sufferings, knowing that suffering produces endurance, and endurance produces character, and character produces hope, and hope does not disappoint us, because God's love has been poured into our hearts (Rom. 5:2-5).

Though the "why" question of suffering is continually probed, its ultimate answer is elusive. Rather, the question becomes a "how" question. "How can I use my suffering with the help of God?" It is very important, though, that whatever use for suffering is found, it be discovered by elders, not imposed on them. This must be the work of codetermination or collaboration, not pastoral imposition.

While this work of collaboration is going on, the elder need not be left to passive endurance of intense pain. Unremitting pain need no longer be the inevitable plight of the elderly. On two fronts great strides have been made in the battle against pain: in pain research and pain clinics and in the hospice movement. In pain research we are learning that pain can be managed through the help of biofeedback devices that enhance mental control. Imaging, in which the sufferer imagines the cells of the body counteracting viruses or malignant cells, engaging them in combat, has also been found helpful in many cases. There are also sophisticated electronic means to dull intractable pain.

In the hospice movement pain-killing drugs, along with intense personal support of the sufferer and family, have been found to be very helpful. Because the medical world is no longer so cautious about drug addiction in those who are terminally ill, there is more freedom to provide the relief that is necessary.

Probing the "why" question

Still the "why" question of suffering will not go away. There is a great need in the human spirit to understand, or at least to make some sense of, suffering. What is particularly agonizing about suffering is the fear that somehow it is evidence of God's displeasure of us or that he has abandoned us. I suspect that what we search for as we ask "Why me, O God?" or "Why this?" is not the answer to suffering, but some assurance that God is not angry with us. We often fear that suffering is evidence that we are still under the nurturing care of God.

Olga S., facing an operation for possible cancer of the ovary, discussed this with her pastor:

Olga: I'm a little depressed. I was supposed to go to surgery this morning, but they cancelled it. I'm still looking at this positively. I wasn't scared when I came in, and I'm not scared now. I have a positive attitude. I have confidence in the doctor. I told him I put God first, and as long as he does what God wills, everything will be OK.

Pastor: God is with you, and I'm sure he is guiding the doctors.

Olga: Yes, I know my life is in God's hands.

She could face a fearful operation, confident that even under anesthesia, her life was in God's hands. This confidence may very well be the reason why the frail elderly have less concern for death, but as the suffering hours and long nights continue, this confidence erodes into wonder whether God has forgotten them.

Is not the question "Why is God letting this happen to me?" really a question that seeks to find out how God feels toward me? When I have pursued the "why" question by asking, "Could you tell me what you think might be the answer?" I have usually gotten a response that reveals the person's perception of their present relationship with God. Often it is concern that the suffering indicates a vindictive God who is angry with them. In older people it may be fear that God has abandoned them, fear sometimes generated by a lifetime of neglect of God and their fellow human beings. Others, who have faithfully endeavored to love God and their neighbors, worry that they have not done enough, so God is dissatisfied with them. Still others, now helpless and no longer able to do anything for God, imagine that God has no more use for them. This fear of abandonment comes through with remarkable regularity in the reports of pastors and students working with the frail elderly.

The providence of God

I am therefore convinced that the providence of God is one of the most vital faith perspectives for older people and that a key pastoral task is the careful development of trust in God's providential care.

There are several ways to understand the providence of God. Most common is a fatalistic resignation, as expressed by one woman waiting beside the deathbed of her husband: "I believe that everyone has a certain time to die. My mother told me that when we are born, there is a candle lit in heaven, and when it goes out, it is our time. When it's Joe's time, nobody can interfere with God's plan." This view puts God in absolute control. God is seen as a kind of cosmic engineer who runs things, the final cause for everything, including even the puzzling tragedies that are so much a part of our personal history. At best, this makes of God a celestial Merlin, who makes everything turn out alright in the end—since God is all-powerful and also good. At worst, it puts forward the impossible question, "How could a loving and all-powerful God permit such a thing to happen?"

Thinking of God as omnipotent *in this sense* is what gets us into trouble. It finally forces the ridiculous question, "Can God make a stone so heavy he can't move it?" The Jewish philosopher Kenneth Seeskin has challenged this view of God's omnipotence. To say that God can do anything is to malign God, for we say this also of most evil persons: "He'll do anything to get his way!" No, God cannot do anything. God cannot lie, steal, cheat, break the promise of his covenant with his people, exhibit cruelty, and a host of other things. The omnipotent God portrayed in biblical texts such as Isaiah 40 is not a cold autocrat, but a God who totally and absolutely transcends all of creation, including our own lives. It is the God portrayed by the Zulu phrase *"Nkosi Nkulu kulu*—the God above gods. But contrary to the Zulu opinion (and most human opinion apart from the revelation of Jesus Christ), this transcendence is *not* indifference to our need. Because God is *beyond* everything, *above it,* so to speak—God can also be in everything. As John A. T. Robinson put it, "God is in the cancer as he is in the sunset, and he is to be met and responded to in each."[2] The ancient Jewish philosopher Maimonedes kept reminding his followers, "His power *is* his goodness, which in turn *is* the infallibility of his will." Rather than to try to understand providence in terms of God's omnipotence, we might better say that God is omnipotent in his compassion.

What the biblical faith asserts is that in and through all the processes of life and history, there is a personal outcome to be faced and a love to be met which nothing, finally, can defeat. This was the faith of Paul (Romans 8). It is more than the hope that God will make everything turn out alright in the end; it is the trust that in everything, no matter what caused it or why it happened, God's Spirit works in us and with us so that even evil may become good. In any and all circumstances, no matter how pointless, those who respond in trust and love are met by the graciousness of God, capable of transforming and liberating even the most baffling events into some meaning and purpose.

After losing my mother, sister, and brother-in-law in a tragic, unexpected flash flood, I attended a worship service in which the congregation sang what is now my favorite hymn: "This Is My Father's World." Somehow the Spirit was able to penetrate my grief—the agonizing, endless, "Why, oh, why?"—with the conviction that even in the raging flood waters there was God—not killing out of some cosmic revenge, but still holding me and the loved ones who were destroyed in loving embrace. Floods, cancer, the wanton killing of drunken drivers—these are not outside the power of God's love. That love is with us *in* those events, just as Jesus Christ was *in* humanity in the cross of Calvary. This is the significance of Isaiah's words: "I form light and create darkness, I make weal and create woe, I am the Lord, who do all these things" (Isa. 45:7).

The doctrine of the providence of God does not describe the designs of God. They are beyond our human understanding. It speaks of the absolute presence of God and God's absolute commitment to redeem the tragedies of life. Even when we cannot find meaning in the event and our why must wait for an answer beyond time, God's love and presence is still there. Both Outler and Robinson contend that the ground of our belief is that the battle is worth our best and that God is calling the shots, that he is also in it, sharing our blows, and that he is going to win the battle for us and for our salvation.[3]

Perhaps we put the issue of providence at the wrong end of our suffering. We tend to ask why as a question about the *origin* and cause of our trauma, when, instead, the question might be put to the *outcome* of life and suffering. This raises the issue of destiny, which is also a part of the providence of God.

Does God have a plan for our lives? Is it all laid out before we are ever born? There are two perspectives for exploring this question. The first is to discover what God desires should happen to us in the ultimate sense. What is our final destiny? The Scriptures are clear on this. It is one of the central themes of the great prophets.

> You shall be my people, and I will be your God. . . . The fierce anger of the Lord will not turn back until he has executed and accomplished the intents of his mind. . . . At that time, says the Lord, I will be the God of all the families of Israel, and they shall be my people. . . . I have loved you with an everlasting love; therefore I have continued my faithfulness to you (Jer. 30:22-24; 31:1-3).

The intent of the mind of God is that no sinner shall die (be ultimately separated from him), but that everyone return to him and be saved. It is this destiny we should remember as the ultimate will of God.

The Danish theologian Regin Prenter called the providence of God "the gospel of creation," by which he meant to say that in whatever befalls us in God's creation, it is God's intention that even the tragic event should in a general way move toward the fulfillment of God's ultimate purpose, the coming kingdom. In a more personal sense, it is God's intention that every tragic event should be redeemed by him and by us in such a way as to enhance, deepen, and strengthen the bond between God, us, and each other. God is then struggling with us to "redeem the time."

Understanding providence as God's working with us to sustain and deepen our relationship with him, ourselves, and others—struggling with us to redeem events and consequences in such a way as to bring blessing—has led some thinkers to understand God's providence most clearly in the attitude of hope. Our hope is in God's compassionate omnipotence coming to us into the present out of the past, and God's redeeming struggling with us, which comes toward us from the future into our present. This transforms even "hopeless suffering" into a destiny that is not destroyed or disfigured by suffering or loneliness, by useless waiting, or even by death. For Christians the ultimate hope is not living without suffering or living a few years longer. Our ultimate hope is in the promise of God: "I never fail you nor forsake you" (Deut. 31:6; Isa. 41:17; Heb. 13:5). Our strength and courage and patience in suffering and through death lie in the assurance of our risen Lord, "Lo, I am with you always, to the close of the age" (Matt. 28:20).

Life review and providence

Almost never do we see the will of God or the providence of God in any direct way. It's more like standing on an ocean liner in the middle of the ocean. Standing on the bow and looking ahead will not tell you the direction of the ship. But move to the stern, see the pattern of the wake, where you have been, and you discover its course. In much the same way one discovers the providential care of God by looking at the wake of our lives.

There is a biblical term that describes this process—*anamnesis*, the remembering of the past events of God's guidance. But *anamnesis* is not merely a recall in the mind. For the ancient people of God and for the New Testament church, *anamnesis* was a replicating and bringing back to life of the recalled experience. Thus for the ancient Hebrews to remember a name of the person was to immediately call forth the person that the name designated. Our acts of remembering the names of family members and friends whom we have lost in death also have this quality. Joshua said to the tribes of Israel, about to enter the promised land, "Remember the word which Moses the servant of the Lord commanded you, 'The Lord your God is providing you a place to rest, and will give you this land' " (Josh. 1:13). Again and again, when Israel was at a critical point in its history, the people were called on to remember the deliverance of God. So the guidance of God was not only brought to mind, but brought into living action in the present moment.

We have a fine example of this sort of remembering in the communion liturgy. The prayer called "The Great Thanksgiving" is such a prayer of remembrance. In it we recall and relive, as it were, God's great, saving acts in response to our Lord's command (1 Cor. 11:24). By this action we bring into the present all that God has done for us. Knowing that God's providence is active in our lives is something like the prayer of Samuel and the people of Israel as they remembered their rescue from the Philistine army and erected a monument named Ebenezer, "Hitherto the Lord has helped us" (1 Sam. 7:12).

The process of life review is strongly recommended as a way of developing a sense of perspective. A life review is like looking at the wake of our life—and seeing the direction of God's guiding, caring nurture. Even if life was bitter, there is evidence that at significant turning points, through little decisions and apparent coincidences, we were led. The loving presence of God was there even in suffering.

The healing effect of such remembrance it vividly portrayed in an excellent film for understanding aging, *Peege*. Through the remembering of her grandson, Peege, who was little more than a "vegetable" in a nursing home, suddenly becomes a person again, a warm, loving grandmother who enjoyed life and loving.

Such a stimulating and guiding *anamnesis* or life review can be one of the most important pastoral contributions a minister can make for the ongoing life of the elderly, particularly the frail elderly. Creative remembering, which recalls the moments of God's guidance, the occasions of joy and love in life, the momentous occasions of decision, can be important in recreating the person of someone who fears abandonment by God and all others. Truly helpful is the life review that concludes, "O God, our help in ages past, Our hope for years to come." Out of this grows trust in the past and hope and courage for the future.

8

Ethical Issues in Aging

Aging raises ethical issues along with the medical, sociological, emotional, and theological issues commonly recognized. Perhaps no other period of human life, with the possible exception of infancy, generates so many ethical concerns. And many of the ethical issues revolve around questions of "quality of life," a prime concern of the Christian community, followers of our Master who declare his destiny: "I came that they may have life, and have it abundantly" (John 10:10). We have a special mandate to be concerned about the ethical aspects of aging.

For the Christian community, ethics and values have something to do with personal relationships. Values and ethics are cherished ideals growing out of and embedded in these relationships, as the commandments themselves arose out of the covenant between God and his people. When ethics are abstracted from these relationships and stand alone as laws, they become harsh, depersonalizing, frequently destroying concern, care, and advocacy.

In the public arena, the primary concern for the aging is *justice.* "Should we not think of justice as including provisions for the well-being of humanity at every stage of the life cycle?" John Bennett has asked.[1]

Institutions and policies of any social order should provide justice for all persons. The claims and counterclaims of the productive and the unproductive are mediated with justice. But because we are human and deal with human beings, justice is raised to higher levels of sensitivity and compassion.

Within the church we perceive that in God's self-revelation in Scripture two primary concerns of God are expressed and developed: God's passion for justice and God's passion for us— God's love. "The Lord loves justice; he will not forsake his saints" (Ps. 37:28). This is expressed most vividly in the prophets, particularly Isaiah: "Behold my servant, whom I uphold, my chosen, in whom my soul delights. . . . He will faithfully bring forth justice. He will not fail or be discouraged till he has established justice in the earth" (Isa. 42:1,3-4). God is concerned that the powerless and the defenseless be the objects of justice rather than oppression, a theme voiced by all the prophets and by Christ himself (Isa. 42:6-7; Luke 4:18-19). Within the confines of the Christian community, sensitivity and compassion become love.

Ethics, particularly as expressed in the twin fundamental principles of justice and love, is a two-way street: we are all responsible under God to give justice as well as to claim the right to justice. So under God we lay claim to compassion and love from others, even as we are bound to give compassion and love. This is no less true of the elderly than it is of persons in the prime of life.

When an oppressed segment of the population has been identified, there is always a danger that we think of justice flowing in only one direction. We are prone to think of justice and compassion directed only to the aged. But they must flow in the opposite direction as well—from the elderly to the community. Only in that way can elders become the true guarantors of a just and humane social order, a true expression of their vocation.

Biblical view of aging

For Christians the Scriptures are the source and norm of faith and life, and their witness indicates the shape and direction of ethical action on the societal as well as the individual level. We turn, therefore, for a brief look at the biblical view of aging.

We must be cautious about too romantic a view of elders in the Bible. Most of the historical books of the Old Testament portray the patriarchs Abraham, Jacob, Saul, David, and Solomon as demonstrating that observation of Solomon's that "there is no man who does not sin" (1 Kings 8:46). The final years of these men were not always beautiful portraits of "the golden years." The Bible avoids the stereotype of equating old age with virtue. Old and young alike are vulnerable, as was Moses when breaking faith with the Lord in old age (Deut. 32:51). Even the book of Job, which displays considerable respect for age ("Wisdom is with the aged, and understanding in length of days" [12:12]), does not equate this with age in any automatic fashion. Elihu's speech (Chapters 32–37) offers a caution against equating quality with quantity of life; what he does suggest, however, is the importance of giving respect to the elders as individuals. The book of Psalms clearly shows that what makes aging a blessing and a source of wisdom is not longevity but fidelity to God; elders should be wise, but even elders can be taught wisdom (Ps. 105:22). "So teach us to number our days that we may get a heart of wisdom" is the prayer for all ages (Ps. 90:12).

The Scriptures see elders from the double perspective of being held in honor and reverence and also as being responsible to society as the source of insight born of experience, wisdom born of faith. In the book of Joshua the elders had this special role, particularly in judging difficult cases (Joshua 20) as they held court at the gates of the city. Seniority seems closely linked with governing power in the early history of Israel, as in most primitive, communal societies.

In the Gospels the most remarkable reference to older people occurs in Luke, whose account opens with the record of Jewish piety out of which John the Baptist and Jesus came, with the stories of Zechariah, Elizabeth, Anna, and Simeon. Pious elders like these are the true conservators of a people, the backbone of the remnant of the faithful.

In the Pauline writings the fundamental principle with respect to age is stated in Gal. 3:28: in Christ there is neither Jew or Greek, slave nor free, male nor female. Following Jesus, Paul recognized human rights and responsibilities to be the universal gifts of God's grace; both saw good and evil in terms of faith and trust in God's redeeming grace, not in any outward distinctions of age or youth, wealth or poverty. Paul did enjoin Timothy to respect the older men and widows in the congregation as "worthy of double honor" (1 Tim. 5:17), and he cautioned against hasty judgment against older persons (1 Tim. 5:19). Special attention was to be given to those older persons who were needy, particularly the widows among the fellowship (1 Tim. 5:3-16). In the letters to Ephesians and Titus, special emphasis is placed on the responsibilities of the older members of the fellowship; parents were not to provoke their children to wrath, and older people were not to give in to slander or to intemperance (Titus 2:2; Eph. 6:1-4). Paul's own aging serves as an example for everyone who ages (which includes just about everybody). This is expressed in his letter to Philemon and the letter to the Philippians, both written by Paul as an old man. His way of facing suffering, imprisonment, setback, frustration, and even death serve as an inspiring and reliable model for us all.

Since the Bible is for us the source and norm for the ethical life, it is well for us to summarize the salient aspects of the biblical understanding of the aged.

1. Elders, like all other persons, were to be respected and honored (Exod. 20:12; Eph. 6:4; Lev. 19:32).

2. The community had reason to expect from seniors wisdom and wise counsel, good judgment. Seniority was a dependable source of wisdom (Lev. 4:15; Deut. 19:12; 21:2; Mark 8:31; Luke 2:25-38; 20:1; Acts 4:5,8,23). This wisdom and good counsel did not automatically come from age, but from trust and obedience to God.

3. The biblical record views as damaging and undesirable any form of generation gap between youth and age. Neither were to be overvalued for their intrinsic qualities. Any stereotype or automatic valuation that would set one age group as preferable over another was to be avoided (Gal. 3:28).

4. Respect for the very young or the very old did not rest on productivity or usefulness, but simply on their existence (Lev. 19:32; Num. 8:23-26).

5. The aged, along with the poor, were to be protected from want and oppression (Acts 6; 1 Timothy 5).

6. The aged, as well as others, were vulnerable to sin; this was not because of their age, but because they turned away from grace. They, too, were called to repentence and were open to change and regeneration just like children (John 3:1-15; Matt. 18:2-4).

We are ready now to look at some of the particular ethical issues especially relevant to the experience of aging. Four groups of ethical problems seem of most relevant concern to pastors: issues of livelihood, issues of personal dignity, issues arising out of health and illness, and issues arising out of dying and death.

Ethical issues in livelihood of the elderly

The foremost issue here is the matter of finances. While it is no longer as true as it once was that older people almost inevitably begin the entry into poverty once they retire, this is a threat to many more elders than should be the case. In his classic work *Aging in America,* Butler noted that six out of every ten older Americans are poor and live below the government-established poverty line. Most become poor after becoming old. Particularly in a time of inflation, aging may, for many people, be an entry into poverty.

Recently I had occasion to visit with a man who had received a large salary during his professional life as pastor of a large and prestigious congregation. He has now been retired for several years. I called to ask him to contribute to a community fund drive. You can imagine his embarrassment and my chagrin at having to hear him detail to me how he and his wife had to cease giving gifts to their family and were being supported in part by their children while living in semipoverty, unable to attend the concerts they enjoyed and unable, though very willing, to contribute to the cause that I represented. What a psychological and emotional shock for anyone who has given his life for family and community in a long and fruitful vocational life to be reduced to this!

Demographers point out that our nation faces some severe social and financial problems in the coming decades as the balance between wage earners and pensioners shifts with the decline in population and increased longevity. How these problems will be solved is still uncertain. Recurrent crises in the Social Security system are the harbingers of the need for some effective long-range solution that looks beyond the "private sector" or a paternalistic government for the answer. Our concern here, however, is recognition of the problem and the importance of justice for all segments of the population.

John Bennett has pointed out two considerations that may encourage young wage earners to accept their part in the support of the elderly.[2]

The first is that the present producers will ultimately become the elderly and will, in all likelihood, live even longer than those now entering retirement. This means that all they now do to support adequate retirement incomes and better conditions of life for the elderly will create and maintain policies from which they will benefit.

The second consideration is that while younger wage earners in many cases have living parents and should feel some responsibility for them, they cannot shoulder this burden by themselves. Most elders do have family, particularly children, who are caring for them in a responsible way to the extent of their ability. It is the heavier burdens of catastrophic illness and adequate space for living that create problems for children supporting their parents. Most young families do not have homes of adequate size to accommodate elders. Moreover, it is better for both young families with children and for grandparents to live detached from each other. The cost of maintaining an elder in a care center can only in rare instances be borne by an individual family without some public assistance.

On the other hand, there is a responsibility resting on pensioners not to be too demanding or greedy. A relative of mine, retired for several years now, has become increasingly disenchanted with some of the advocacy groups made up of older people. He is particularly irritated when the "grey lobby" absolutely refuses to consider any change in the cost of living index that elevates Social Security benefits. Elders have a responsibility to avoid confusing their wants with real needs, demanding greater financial support than the economy can bear.

The issue here is justice—for elders and for wage earners. Martin Heinecken has said that "younger persons must show compassion by being willing to shoulder a greater but equitably distributed tax burden."[3] Tax revolts and careful monitoring of taxes of all forms to counter wasteful government spending and inequities are always in order. "But the revolt," Heinecken went on to say, "will itself be grossly unjust if it succeeds at the expense of the aged or some other already-oppressed minority."

In 1978 the Lutheran Church in America adopted a human-rights statement similar to that adopted by many other denominations, which declares that "parents are entitled to respect, affection and care from their children" and "older adults are entitled to the opportunity to continue as participating members of society and should not be denied, because of circumstances beyond their control, adequate housing, sustenance or health care."

Dignity of life

Concern for dignity and respect is common to all ages. Children require respect, as do parents and elders. Men as well as women are to be regarded as persons. The biblical and theological foundations for this concern are quite clear: all persons are created in the image of God, which is to say not only that they stand in special relationship to God, but that by creative acts and continued involvement in the creation of the world God has irrevocably committed himself to humanity. Any treatment of any human being that does not consider this foundation and ultimate destiny fails to respect the dignity of that person and is an affront to God, the Creator and Redeemer. It is this created and redeemed relationship that makes and keeps us human, no matter what age, and it is to this center that we must gravitate when outward events—particularly the debilitating and depersonalizing aspects of the closing months or years of life—tend to make us treat persons as objects.

In caring for those with whom it is often difficult or impossible to communicate, or with persons who seem to take no cognizance of us, it is easy to begin to think of these people as "objects of care" or, even worse, as "vegetables"—no longer as persons. When we visit the frail elderly in nursing facilities or hospitals, we can help counteract this tendency by thinking of them as if they were our grandmother, or elderly uncle, or perhaps aged parents. To see them in the context of a personal relationship enables us to recognize their humanity. To see their personal relationship with God helps restore our attitude of *agape* caring.

Dealing with the elderly—in whatever circumstances—simply as cases or objects to be treated or taken care of is a violation of fundamental ethics of aging. Roger Shinn has noted some of the forces in our modern society that tend to erode our dignity and depersonalize us. One of these is the ever greater coordination and social control required in a complex, technological society. This includes the care of the frail elderly by means of technological medicine. The increasing number of frail elderly in our population will only exacerbate this situation.

The erosion of dignity results from the loss or even the usurping of a person's decision-making power. The retention of this power as long as it can be exercised is highly important to one's sense of personhood or autonomy. Personal autonomy *alone* is not the primary ethical value Christian pastoral care of elders would preserve; to assert this would be to undercut the importance of personal relationships. It is interrelated autonomy— autonomy within the matrix of responsible relationships to God, family, and society—that we seek to preserve. And this involves the right and responsibility of the individual to make choices whenever possible. Our first preference should always be to allow individual persons to make their own choices, and only when this is manifestly impossible, unwise, or dangerous to life, should this value be infringed upon. Personal choices by elders, however, are not to be made in self-concerned isolation, but always in the matrix of interrelationships in which we stand under God, in relation to our families, our friends, and the larger community. This becomes an important aspect of pastoral guidance in decision making. It is one of the chief pitfalls of agism to assume that the older persons get, the less able they are to fulfill interrelated autonomy.

Dignity involves choosing where one shall live, how one shall be treated in that living arrangement, what medical treatment should be given, and finally, how one shall die and perhaps even *when* one shall die. The Social Statement of Death and Dying passed by the Lutheran Church in America in 1982 effectively articulates this principle:

> If the person is capable of actively participating in the decision-making process, respect for that person [the elder] mandates that he or she be recognized as the prime decision maker.

The document continues:

> If the patient has the prime decision-making role, the question then becomes one of the refusing treatment for one's self. . . . Since our responsibilities for stewardship of our own lives do not differ significantly from our responsibilities for the lives of others, the general guidelines outlined . . . are pertinent here. Thus, for example, one may in good conscience refuse burdensome treatment in some situations.

The issue of treating or caring for a person in a manner that is against their wishes raises the issue of self-determination:

> To treat a patient (or person) in violation of his or her deeply held, carefully considered, and clearly expressed preference is to do violence to that person just as surely as would physically assaulting that person.

> In all cases—including those situations in which a person's considered judgments are unmistakably clear—there is a continuing responsibility to care for and to extend the warmth of human community.

While the context for this document is medical care, the principles apply also to other decisions and forms of caring. Almost every family with a frail elderly member struggles with the difficult matter of "How long shall grandma (or grandpa) be permitted to live all alone?" The principle to be followed is clear, even though the execution of it may be difficult for a loving family to accept: as long as she (or he) is able to enter rationally and intelligently into the decision, as long as she takes into account the whole network of her relationships and those related to her, it is her decision. I am sure that if our elders felt that we as their children, well-meaning friends, and pastors were committed to this principle, they would much more willingly enter into dialog with us about what decision to make. It is their fear that we are going to take over their lives and make their decisions for them that makes them reluctant—just as teenagers are—to take us into their confidence as they reflect on what to decide.

Another ethical issue growing out of a concern for the respect and dignity of persons is the matter of privacy. Privacy is intimately related to one's responsibility and right to make one's own decisions, and both are important aspects of self-esteem and personal identity. Privacy is a cultural variable, more highly valued among us than in more communal cultures, where the sense of personhood depends much more on being in close proximity with others. Thus the importance of privacy for a person of Hispanic background is different than for Anglos, and, to the extent that black persons are still related to archetypal communal cultures of Africa, it is valued differently than for most middle-class Americans. Privacy is carefully guarded in our national constitution and in statutory law as a fundamental human right. But like the responsibility and right of personal decision, this, too, rapidly erodes with aging. Old age somehow seems to render one's personal affairs and even one's personal processes public, ranging all the way from financial affairs at the time of entry into a care center to one's bodily processes in a skilled nursing facility.

To grant an elder her or his privacy is to counteract the discriminating and depersonalizing effects of agism in a particularly effective way. By respecting the privacy of persons you are granting them individuality and seeing them as unique and as individuals, not simply as part of a stereotyped group.

One strand of agism that relates especially to privacy is the matter of sexual feelings and sexual expression. The stereotype has it that old people are sexless, almost as if they were becoming a third gender—old. This finds expression in the difficulty that most nursing homes have with sexuality. Even married couples are often separated from each other in poorly managed nursing homes that give no attention to personal privacy. In the living arrangement of older people, particularly the frail elderly, we ought carefully to consider by what right we can interfere with the private affairs of any couple, of whatever age. To the end of life sexuality is a beautiful gift of God to be enjoyed in private.

The aspect of privacy that a pastor has special responsibility for is confidentiality. The content of pastoral conversations, even when they are not of a confessional nature, ought to be respected. This means that concerns an elder shares with a pastor are not later to be shared with other members of the family without the consent or knowledge of the elder. Somehow we assume that very old people have become children, and we treat confidences of elders as if they are of no particular moment and can be shared with anyone. Pastors should be particularly cautious that they do not allow this attitude of infantilization to take over, especially toward the frail elderly.

These cautions are particularly important when a pastor is caring for a multigenerational family in which a middle-aged couple is parenting aged parents or grandparents. In such a setting, confidences shared by any of the individuals must not be shared with others without permission. In those instances in which it seems necessary to share vital information with the primary caregiver in a family, it is wise and ethical to get the permission of the elder to do so, explaining why it is important that the information be shared. In such an intergenerational setting an important pastoral function is to open up and maintain mutual trust and communication. This is easily destroyed by inattention to confidentiality.

Elder abuse

A phenomenon which apparently is on the increase, but has only recently begun to attract public attention, is elder abuse. This refers to violence against elderly persons by various caretakers, usually within their families. Elder abuse is likely to be on the increase as the population becomes older and finances force more older persons to be cared for within their families.

Research studies on those older persons who are not being cared for in nursing homes indicate that about 10% of the dependent elderly are at risk of abuse from family members in one form or another. Very probably one of the greatest sources of abuse is from family members who are caretakers in a situation in which generational reversal has taken place: middle-aged or older children are cast in a parental role, caring for their frail elderly parents. Currently, about half of the people now over age 65 who have living children are members of four-generation families.

Several family dynamics contribute to elder abuse. As with child or spouse abuse, victimized elders are dependent on the abusers for basic care. They bear the further burden of a sense of guilt for having raised a child who now mistreats them. Secondly, it turns out that women are both the predominant victims of abuse and are at the same time abusers. Abuse is generated out of the sense of helplessness of the caregiver, sometimes due to the intractability of the elder, or because the elder is victim of age-related diseases such as stroke, Alzheimer's disease, or from mood-altering medication. One caregiver expressed her dilemma in these words: "My elderly mother won't contribute to the household costs. I'm making a woman's salary and keeping a big house. It's an obligation she should partly assume. She doesn't feel that way. I'm her daughter; she provided for me when I was young, and now the obligation rests on my shoulders." This woman of 68 attributed the breakup of her marriage to the intractability of her elderly mother. Often conflict arises out of misapplication of the commandment "Honor your father and your mother." Forgotten is the corresponding ethical responsibility of parents, articulated by Paul, "Fathers do not provoke your children to anger" (Eph. 6:4).

Many caregivers of elderly parents, grandparents, or even great-grandparents are themselves caught between two or more generations. They have a double burden and frequent ethical dilemmas. Whose needs take priority, those of one's children (usually teenagers or young adults) or those of the elderly? The frustration of attempting to resolve these dilemmas, often alone, gives rise to violence and abuse of elders.

Abuse and violence can take a double direction: violence perpetrated on elders by their children easily attracts our attention, but often hidden is the counterviolence of elders on their caregivers. One caregiver, a woman of 64, was unable to leave her home because whenever she did so, her 94-year-old father would violently attack her and turn the house into a shambles.

Violence is not always physical. It can be psychological or even spiritual means used to manipulate or force a person to act or cease from acting in ways that are unacceptable to the abuser. Screaming and yelling are the most common forms, but physical restraint, use of force in feeding or medication, or a threat to send the elder to a nursing home are forms most often used against elders. Elders also use varied means of violence against caregivers, such as a threat to stop eating or taking medicine, exploitation of one's physical or emotional disability ("Oh, my heart!"), and the use of physical force.

Parish pastors or congregational members are often the first persons to become aware of elder abuse. This provides both a real opportunity and a serious responsibility for appropriate intervention. Often there is not a great deal that a pastor or pastoral caregivers can do directly to prevent violence. Indirectly, there is much that can be done. Providing support for those under strain and frustration is important. Offering a means of talking it out rather than acting it out can be helpful. In doing this, it is important, however, that a pastor avoid taking sides, no matter how tempting it might be to do so. Avoid especially the natural tendency to side with the elder against the caregivers. By remaining more or less neutral, a pastor can more effectively function as a mediator, stimulating dialog to explore alternate solutions to the problems. A pastor should only rarely become an accuser, and never a condemner.

Another important contribution pastors can make is to clarify ethical principles and commandments, particularly misunderstandings and misapplications of the commandment to "honor thy father and mother," pointing out that Scripture assumes mutual responsibilities. A pastor is often the only person in a tense family situation who can speak pointedly to elders about their responsibilities to children and to family, provided he or she has maintained some objectivity in the situation.

Pastors can also be of help in exploring alternatives for eldercare. Congregations can often be mobilized to provide assistance or relief for overburdened caregivers. An occasional holiday away from family, in the home of others, can be most beneficial for an elder and a caregiver.

Minority elders

Ageism is itself a form of discrimination and therefore to be deplored and corrected in whatever way possible. The elderly also experience racial discrimination. The plight of the black elderly should not be overlooked by pastors serving inclusive congregations. For some blacks, being one of the middle-old or frail elderly will not be much different than for most whites, especially insofar as they have begun to experience the benefits and liabilities of being a part of the middle class in America. Thurman F. is a retired social worker, and he and his wife live comfortably on his pension. Now 73, Thurman has been active as a volunteer in a number of community organizations. His life is not much different from that of most white, middle-class retirees.

But Harriet J. has been self-supporting since she was 12. She works as a domestic and caterer. She, too, is 73. She gets some Social Security, but it's not enough to maintain her (domestics don't usually build up Social Security accounts), so she continues to work and expects to do so until she dies. She can't afford to retire. That is perhaps more common among blacks than among whites. Economic and health considerations are uppermost for people who continue to suffer job and financial discrimination as they grow older.

In many black communities, family and kinship structures have in the past been able to provide a modicum of care, particularly for elderly, black women. These structures are breaking down, however, causing many older blacks to be entirely without social-support resources. Also, blacks are frequently so isolated from the social and legal systems that they are unaware of the resources that might provide help.

Churches and pastors ought to make themselves aware of the plight of minority elders in their communities and seek to make support systems available to them. There is also the responsibility for urban churches, especially, to be on the alert for elderly members, often living on a pittance, who are hidden in one-room flats all over the inner city. Through clergy and volunteers, congregations may need to provide emergency social services for such persons, but congregations ought also to see to it that the systems of our society are opened to these persons. An advocacy role is clearly in order.

Abuse of drugs among elderly

Chemical abuse, alcoholism, and drug dependency are currently reaching alarming proportions among our aging population. We see it in two forms: alcohol addiction and the unwarranted use of drugs in care and treatment. Of the various forms of drug abuse, some regard alcoholism as the most serious. According to recent statistics, there are more than three million alcoholics over the age of 60 in the U.S. Alcohol abuse is highest among elderly widowers. As always, chemical abuse is both a personal health and life-style problem as well as a social commentary. What is there about the life and outlook of those over 60 that generates dependency on drugs?

One area that is not often given sufficient attention is the amount of stress to which those over 65 are subjected. If you compound giving up an occupational life and life-style, moving to a new home, the loss of friends or spouse in death or by moving, financial stress, and add physical pain and anxiety, it is easy to understand why older people live under at least as much stress as a junior executive or young adult. Our cultural response to stress is alleviation by drugs, and the elderly are no exception. In addition to stress, loss of meaning for living, increased inactivity, and leisure may also generate alcoholism, particularly in retirement communities, where alcohol abuse is becoming a major problem.

A closely related ethical problem is the increasing tendency of the medical and nursing home community to use mood-altering drugs as a means of social control and treatment, especially with the frail elderly. Keeping people completely or partially tranquilized makes them easier to manage and less trouble for the staff. In one study, tranquilizers accounted for 35% of the medication prescribed for Medicare patients in Illinois, Ohio, and New Jersey. Excessive use of tranquilizers sometimes causes older people to feel that they are losing control of their memory, vision, and physical abilities more rapidly than is actually true. It has been found that excessive tranquilization and the interaction of too many different drugs stimulates behavior that leads to the false diagnosis of "senility"; when such people are taken off drugs the "senile" behavior disappears. Elders who are too heavily drugged are also artificially isolated from human interaction, which might otherwise keep them more alert and mentally and spiritually healthy. Misuse of drugs in this manner is more frequently found in the proprietary nursing home, which by definition has divided loyalties between care for persons and making a profit. Therefore it is important for pastors and congregations to be on the alert for such misuse wherever there are frail elderly who present management problems.

As with so many of the other ethical issues arising out of aging, pastoral and congregational alertness to the possibilities of misuse are called for. Once unwholesome dependency or abuse of drugs has been discovered, three strategies seem most useful. First, through pastoral initiative and communal support, encourage the person to get proper medical care. If alcoholism is involved, treatment should best be in a group setting. Second, it is helpful to do everything possible to increase wholesome social contacts for the elderly person through involvement in church and community social life (where possible) or more intentional visitations of the homebound person. Finally, it is important to try to remove or alleviate the factors that generate the drug misuse. This may mean more careful attention to providing continuing meaning for life, more precise and careful management of pain, relief of financial stress, and appropriate care for persons who are bereaved.

Though our stereotypes of agism do not permit us to think of older persons as alcoholics or drug abusers, realities require us to face the fact that this is likely to become an increasing problem for the elderly. It is also a concern to be addressed by the church.

Crime against the elderly

Public-opinion polls dealing with the concerns of older people report that one of the top-ranking fears is the fear of criminal assault. Since more than 60% of the nation's elderly live in the central city, where crime rates are the highest, and since elderly people are more defenseless, these fears are justified. Of the forms of crime that anger us most as a society, crimes against the elderly rank very high; they offend our sense of justice more profoundly than many other forms of injustice.

The effect of this widespread fear of crime on the elderly is undue social isolation. Elders cringe behind locked doors at night and forego the benefits of cultural events, social gatherings, and church attendance. Every urban pastor knows the difficulty, or even impossibility, of planning evening events to which elders are encouraged to come.

Victims over 65 suffer greater consequences from crime than do younger people. The financial loss from theft, the most common form of crime, can be catastrophic. Rarely can they afford insurance to cover a loss. Psychologically, the effect is equally damaging and can leave a victim with a sense of violation, threat, and fear for the remainder of life. The effects of physical injury resulting from crime are obvious, especially for the vulnerable, frail elderly. It is a situation demanding the attention of the church and our nation.

Congregations can establish care networks and telephone contacts, provide alarm systems, and stimulate police activity to stem this trend. This and other ethical issues arising out of aging need not be laid only at the feet of a pastor or lay caregiver, but can often be effectively dealt with by elders themselves. No greater fulfillment of Christian vocation can be imagined than continued service to the larger community in such a manner. Pastoral leadership, imagination, and encouragement are often all that is needed to generate such a response. The National Institute of Law Enforcement and Criminal Justice recognizes the following advantages in having older volunteers contribute to the criminal justice system:

• Older volunteers are generally supportive of the criminal justice system and are available because of their time and interest.

• Older volunteers often have needed skills or are already trained or readily trainable.

• Older volunteers are usually dependable and conscientious, exhibiting high workmanship and ethical standards.

• Older volunteers can perform valuable community-relations services as they become advocates of the agency. They can also perform valuable services in traffic control, communications, prisoner service, block-watch programs, security surveys, and a host of other areas.

Dealing more realistically and effectively with crime against the elderly is clearly an important responsibility to which the church must contribute by consciousness raising, clear moral leadership, and direct action.

Ethical issues and responsibilities do not cease with retirement, but remain with us as long as life remains. They change with the new challenges and opportunities of aging, and for some become more complex and puzzling. The pastor is, or could be, a most significant person to assist families and their elders in working through the issues that confront them.

Inappropriate commitment to mental hospitals

It has often been the case that older persons have been inappropriately placed in a mental hospital under the assumption that they were "hopelessly senile," or even as a way of getting a troublesome or cantankerous elder out of the way. Fortunately, due to recent efforts to reduce the number of chronic mental patients in these hospitals, this no longer happens quite so regularly. Often, however, the motive to deinstitutionalize is purely economic rather than familial or societal altruism.

Such commitments are often made out of a misdiagnosis of senility, when in fact the bizarre and intractable behavior was due to what is now recognized as acute brain syndrome, which is reversible. But it does sometimes happen that a person who is not truly mentally ill is committed, adjudged legally incompetent, and a conservator or guardian is appointed by the probate court to assume management of the person's affairs. Bereft of all legal rights, the "incompetent person" is often stripped of home, possessions, and financial responsibility. This can happen without any malicious intent, yet our theological awareness of the true nature of human beings ought to make us as suspect of even our most altruistic motives. Recently society itself has begun to recognize this in the form of the beneficial drive toward "patient's rights" in both general and mental hospitals. Pastors and members of Christian congregations ought always to be champions of such patient rights, as part of our intent to be loving and compassionate.

In order to protect our elders from injustice of this sort, moves to declare someone mentally incompetent (legally insane) ought to be made with extreme caution. Thorough medical, neurological, and psychiatric evaluation are to be insisted upon, and second opinions should be made mandatory. Proper legal procedures should be followed when a person is committed to a mental hospital, and even more care should be exercised in the appointment of guardians or conservators by the court. Normally it is unwise for a pastor to serve as such a court-appointed officer, since it may lead to conflicts of interest. But pastors and the members of a congregation may fulfill an important "watchdog" role to make sure that the well-being and the expressed wishes of the elder are carefully balanced with wishes of family and relatives, particularly if they are potential financial heirs.

The ethical dilemmas of aging can be among the most difficult ones we face. Pastoral sensitivity to these issues can be most helpful in providing ministry to older persons in the congregation. What guides us both as elders and as caring pastors is compassion and justice, concern for quality of life, and freedom from oppression and the erosion of dignity and responsibility. In this chapter we have sought to alert pastors to special ethical problems involved in growing older against this backdrop of justice and compassion.

9

Facing the Dilemmas of Dying

Among the most difficult ethical issues related to aging are those dealing with the closing days and hours of life. In these moments questions are raised by the elder patient, members of the family, and the medical profession that require the wisdom of one greater than Solomon. Yet they must be dealt with, even though they can hardly ever be answered to everyone's satisfaction. Here we need to walk cautiously and with trust in the mercy of God. In the ethical dilemmas that are raised in these moments, there is quite often no answer that is absolutely morally "right"; we may have to arrive at solutions that contain elements of self-concern and sin along with that which is right. We need, then, to pray in utter repentance that the destructiveness of our self-concern be held at a minimum as we depend on God's mercy.

In this chapter we will identify particular ethical issues that surround our pilgrimage through death and provide some opportunity for reflection on those issues (without the thoroughgoing ethical analysis that is inappropriate in a book of this type). It is hoped that perspectives will emerge that will assist in clarifying the agonizing decisions that have to be made.

Death with dignity

Today family members, physicians, nurses, hospital personnel, and even the political community are becoming more sensitive to the issues involved in dying with dignity. Often a pastor stands right in the middle, seeking to communicate with all, keeping the channels of communication and concern open, providing support, and stimulating reflection.

To go on living or to surrender to dying—that is the dilemma for many an elder. It's not that the aged hate life. Almost everyone clings to life and does everything possible to ward off death, but finally there comes a time when it just doesn't seem worth the struggle anymore. The continued suffering, the loneliness, the loss of purpose and meaning finally begin to corrode the precious jewel of living. That's the situation Anna, a 77-year-old widow with no children, faced. She had had a colostomy and also suffered from the effects of a recent stroke. She lived in a geriatric hospital and spoke with difficulty to the pastor visiting her.

Pastor: The nurse's aid told me that last week you went on a trip down to the hills.

Anna: (*Speaking slowly*) Oh yes! It was nice . . . it was nice. (*A long pause while she tries to speak, but can't.*)

Pastor: How did you go to the hills? (*Silence.*) What did they do about your noon meal?

Anna: (*Slowly*) They sent it along with us . . . . We . . . ate . . . together. (*A long pause*) You know I used to be quite a talker. I used to talk all the time. (*Pause.*) Why don't you go and visit someone else? There are other people here who can just talk a blue streak.

Pastor: But I came to see you. Would you rather I come another time?

Anna: (*Another long pause and then she finally says*) My niece was here to see me today and she brought along my grand-nephew. Here is his picture. (*She pauses again.*) Sometimes I just wish I could die.

Pastor: What do you mean?

Anna: Everyone here is just put here to die. I just know it. That's why everyone is here in this hospital. (*A pause, and she sighs.*) I just wish I could die. You know my husband is dead. I'm the only one left. . . . There just doesn't seem to be any reason to live.

There are many people who, like Anna, are just waiting for death to take them. Like her, they may wonder why God doesn't hurry up. When our lives have lost meaning for ourselves and for others, then we begin to wonder and to wish for life to end.

Dr. Albert Outler, in reflecting on his life and on dying, has commented in a similar vein:

> Death is, I take it, the ultimate deprivation. I worry a great deal, for I do not see how to insure a graceful exit. This is the remaining problem . . . what is the chance of a graceful exit? The degree of indignity that comes with old age and helplessness, the dependence upon and bother to others seems to me to be graceless. This I dread more than anything I can identify. . . . Getting out of life is more difficult than getting in—certainly for the person himself or herself. But as for what it will take to insure this, I do not know.[1]

That, for many, is a difficult question.

There is a strong tradition that says that God alone has the right to give life and to take it. Most elders will remember the phrase, "The Lord giveth, the Lord taketh away, blessed be the name of the Lord" (Job 1:21 KJV). Often remembering this is the only thing that prevents an elder from simply giving up on life, or even actively taking steps to terminate it.

Not so clear anymore is the issue of just who has this responsibility. Is it the Lord God, or the lord physician with drugs and tubes and pumps and respirators and ventilators and pacemakers and electronic stimulators? Just when does the time come when the process of living becomes a process of dying that should be transferred to the hands of God? Medical terminology has served to extend this question rather than to answer it; often the more remarkable the advances of life-saving techniques, the more difficult the answers.

Most pastors have heard the familiar question, "Is it right to pray that I might die?" Is it responsible action under God to consider how far the limited resources of medical skill, money, hospital space, and equipment should be extended just to preserve life for a few more months, days, or maybe hours? Is it right to take into account the quality of living that these extended moments provide? How much import should the feelings of the family, the community, and society have in my decision about my "death with dignity"?

And in the midst of all of this, what kind of guidance can the church give? A pastor often stands right in the middle, with questions pouring in from everyone involved. The moral tradition of the Western churches has been almost uniform in its opposition to suicide and euthanasia, or mercy killing. However, this rigid opposition is beginning to erode as technological medicine heightens the dilemmas. The seemingly unlimited extension of terminal illness by technological means requires that distinctions be made between mere quantity of life and quality of living: mere passivity is no longer possible. We just don't let nature take its course anymore.

Leadership in these areas has been given by the Roman Catholic Church, with its long tradition of moral theology. In 1957 a breakthrough occurred when Pope Pius XII pronounced that it was acceptable to withhold life supports from some patients who were incurable, in coma, or in hopeless pain. This was reiterated again in 1980 in a Vatican statement: "When inevitable death is imminent, patients may refuse forms of treatment that would only secure a precarious and burdensome prolongation of life."[2] Both the American Lutheran Church and the Lutheran Church in America, along with most other Protestant denominations, have taken similar stands. An LCA document of 1982 states:

> There comes a time to recognize the reality of what is happening by refraining from attempts to resuscitate the person and by discontinuing the use of artificial life support systems. To try desperately to maintain the vital signs of an irreversibly dying person, for whom death is imminent, is inconsistent with a Christian ethic that mandates respect for dying as well as for living.[3]

This document speaks straightforwardly of respect for dying, as for living, and of the importance of "death with dignity." I would argue against any presumed *right* to death with dignity; it seems to be more a matter of responsibility and opportunity, both for the dying person and for those surrounding him or her.

Before we proceed much further, it is helpful to keep in mind some distinctions in the manner of intervention with living or dying. There is a continuum to be considered. At one end is the most passive action of the dying person (such as refusing to eat or take medicine) or the physician simply not undertaking new treatment. In the middle is a more active intervention, such as withdrawing treatment already under way; this falls into the category of "passive euthanasia." The next, and far more radical, step is "active euthanasia," in which there is deliberate intervention to hasten death. At the far end of the continuum is suicide, which has several levels (to be discussed later).

The LCA document provides the helpful additional distinction between three types of persons being treated: the irreversibly dying person; patients for whom a particular treatment is extremely burdensome and reduces quality of life; and chronically ill individuals, for whom intense chronic pain and suffering are the special concern. Aged persons can be identified in any of these categories.

As one considers death with dignity, the decisions about continuing treatment or types of treatment that are appropriate, families, elder patients, physicians, and often pastors must struggle to find an appropriate balance between the treatment to be used, its degree of complexity or risk, its cost, and the possibility of using it—comparing these elements with the anticipated result, taking into account the emotional and spiritual state of the particular elder patient, the family, and their mutual moral, physical, and economic resources. For an older person in the church, for the family, and for the pastor, the context for all of this decision making is "the fear and love of God," in reverence of God and the gift of life. Such "fear of God" is indeed "the beginning of wisdom" (Ps. 111:10).

Luther began his explanation of the Fifth Commandment with a contrast to the negative of the commandment: "We should fear and love God. . . . " Such fear or reverence for God expresses itself in reverence for life and reverence for dying as well. Christians should remember that "whether we live or whether we die, we are the Lord's" (Rom. 14:8).

Respect for life

To respect life is to cherish it as a gift from a loving Creator. To cherish life is to preserve and protect it under all normal circumstances; it is as if every Christian lived under the most stringent Hippocratic oath. To cherish life is to be concerned not just about its longevity, but about its quality as well. Life under God is more than breathing through hours and days; it is responsive loving, caring and being cared for, serving and being served, being creative and graceful, appreciated and appreciating others. When we cherish a gift, we hold it dear not because of its intrinsic value but because it expresses the love of someone who loves us and whom we love. It may not be a perfect gift, it may not even have great utility, but we cherish it because of the giver. For Christians, this puts to rest questions about the "meaningfulness" or "usefulness" of life; whether or not elders (or anyone else) is "useful" ought never to be a major consideration in the decisions of death, with or without dignity.

To cherish life is to receive God's gift of life responsibly. Responsible cherishing means that we are constantly called upon to make decisions about longevity and quality, rather than refrain lest we be "playing God." The times when we play God are not only at the time of deciding to "pull the plug." They begin when a parent takes an infant for vaccination and continue through life as we seek to preserve and care for our neighbor's body and life through various kinds of medical intervention.

In considering the matter of responsible stewardship of life in the face of dying, we are in the domain of *right* and *responsibility*. As the public media report these issues, they tend to speak in terms of *right*: the right to death with dignity, the right to refuse treatment, or the right to life. We need to bear in mind that this is fundamental legal language, the common bedrock on which we all as citizens live and think. And because we live in a world in which all people tend to be self-seeking, we are sometimes forced to defend our rights, even at the expense of the rights of others. But simply to insist on my rights can often be destructive to one's self and to others. For Christians the matter does not end with insisting on our individual rights; in fact the issue is not the self-protection of personal right, rather our right and responsibility is to defend our *neighbor's* rights. Our concern for justice is not that *we* have justice, but that justice be done to *all*, particularly to our neighbor, and especially to our neighbor who is oppressed. Thus, for Luther, one of the most honorable of all professions was politics, in which a Christian could be active in the defense of his (or her) neighbor's rights.

When we clutch our individual rights to our breasts, like threatened children, we set the stage for adversary medicine and the prevalence of litigation, which has done so much to escalate the costs of care. A responsible concern for the rights of others, regardless of what may happen to our own rights, would do much to reduce the cost and threat of catastrophic medical care.

The issue of whether to withhold treatment, and the more interventionist one of withdrawing treatment in the interests of death with dignity, has recently been given wide circulation. Fundamental to this matter is the "right" of the patient to be involved in the decision-making process. There is considerable ethical difference between providing the context in which a person can make an informed decision and deciding for that person. There are also different legal implications. Respect for the dignity of elders requires that we respect their right—or better, their responsibility—to make these decisions as they are capable; but to expect that elder persons possibly facing death can make such decisions all alone is to fail to respect and cherish them.

It is also appropriate that older persons making decisions about their death make them not simply out of consideration for what they wish, but also take into account the wishes and needs of their family and the larger community. In the face of constantly rising medical costs, the impact that catastrophic illness might have, and the implications for Christian stewardship, I have considered making a "living will" statement that limits the amount of money that can be expended on my terminal medical care; but as I think about this, I must take into account the wishes of my family and the effect such a decision might have on them.

A chaplain told of a widow in her late 70s who was admitted to the hospital several times for treatment of congestive heart failure. Each time she was treated successfully and returned home with the instructions to avoid salt. Within a short time she

would be back in the hospital with accumulated fluids and short-
ness of breath, having totally ignored her physician's advice. In
one admission she was even discovered to have hidden salt in
her overnight case. Since she seemed so obstinate about treatment and did not respond to the doctor's persuasion, the chaplain was asked to talk with her. He found her a winsome, lonely
person. Her husband had died several years earlier, and her
children, now married, were on their own. She did not seem to
be close to any of them. Frequently she would sigh and remark,
"All I have left now is my Lord." When the chaplain commented
on her loneliness, she said, "Oh, I'm not lonely. I have my Lord."
Yet it was clear she felt alone in the world and was ready to die.
In considering these details, the medical staff concluded that by
refusing to follow dietary regulations, she was deliberately has-
tening her own longed-for death. For her, death meant relief
from the burden of loneliness and a reunion with her husband
and her Lord.

There are many elders who in this fashion make and carry
out their decision. To us on the sidelines, it might seem to be an
acceptable one. But in order to determine that fully, we would
want to consider the impact of such a decision on her family.
For many elders, death with dignity is anticipated and somewhat
protected with the living will, a document that many states now
recognize as valid instructions to physicians and family in the
event of terminal illness. The living will simply stipulates that no
extraordinary means be undertaken to prolong life or intervene
with the dying process; in hospital parlance it is the "no code"
decision. In the event of onset of death, no emergency measures
for resuscitation are to be undertaken.

Decisions in this regard are difficult to make, and, whenever
possible, members of the family as well as other, more objective
advisors such as the chaplain, pastor, physician, and close family
friends should be involved. It is always better to make such decisions before the crisis occurs. Decisions made in pitch of a crisis
are not always wise and may later be regretted.

Even in dying, elders still have the possibility—if not the responsibility—to continue the role of being the conservators of
life, as they have been conservators of love, faith, and hope in
their lifetimes. This can be done by designating one's body as a

gift to medical science for research and study, an act that might have lifesaving value for one's grandchildren as well as others. One can designate one's body as a source for donor organs insofar as their physical condition permits. One can also leave instructions with one's family and physician for an autopsy to be performed after death, which in itself can help to extend medical and scientific knowledge and wisdom. Pastoral reflection, encouragement, and support can be of vital significance as these decisions are contemplated.

Suicide

A few years ago the ecumenical religious community was shocked to hear of the death of Dr. H. P. Van Dusen and his wife. Dr. Van Dusen, one of the founders of the World Council of Churches and president of Union Theological Seminary from 1945 to 1963, died within a few days of the death of his wife. His wife suffered from severe arthritis, and Dr. Van Dusen had suffered a severe stroke five years before his death, which greatly hindered his physical activity and prevented him from speaking normally. The two had engaged in a suicide pact rather than face the prospect of further enfeebling old age. During the night in which they acted on their pact, he vomited the overdose of sleeping pills he had taken, but he died of heart failure 15 days later.

Professor J. T. Bennett, a prominent ethicist and close friend of the Van Dusens for over 40 years, wrote of the incident: "When I first heard about it, my only thought was an intensified feeling of sorrow for the years of suffering that had brought two friends . . . to such a decision. I knew that I could not even imagine the difficulty of making this decision. Nothing was further from my mind than the idea of sitting in judgment on what they had done."[4] In his ethical and theological reflection on the event, Bennett further wrote, "I agree with those who say that the chief approach to the problems of death in life . . . should be emphasis on passive euthanasia, or the refusal to take extraordinary measures to preserve life." I agree with this conclusion, as well as with Dr. Bennett's grave reluctance to sit in judgment on such a momentous decision, one not made lightly but with grace and careful awareness of the moral issues involved.

With respect to the matter of self-administered euthanasia or suicide, the general consensus of Christendom is with the statement of Dietrich Bonhoeffer: "God has reserved to himself the right to determine the end of life, because he knows the goal to which it is his will to lead it."[5] Yet Bonhoeffer went on to say that there might be situations in which a sufferer of an incurable disease, whose prolonged treatment would bring nothing but added suffering and material and psychological ruin of the family, might make a decision that would free them from this burden. "Then no doubt there are many objections to such unauthorized action; and yet here, too, a condemnation will be impossible."

We have been assuming here a particular form of suicide or self-administered euthanasia, which Dr. Bennett in another context called "terminal suicide," and which is far different from the suicide of a young man disappointed in love. Ethically there is a close relationship here with the self-sacrifice that brings death, such as Dietrich Bonhoeffer himself engaged in (or as is common on the battlefield), so one must be reluctant to be the ready condemner.

Both Bennett and Stanley Heuerwas have made the important point that neither "terminal suicide" nor any form of euthanasia ought to become an example for other persons, nor a norm for society.[6] On this ground, then, one must vehemently disagree with those groups such as EXIT (in Great Britain) that go to the extent of providing instructions for the "best" forms of suicide. One is impelled to assert the conclusions of most churches that formalized euthanasia is to be resisted. In such a stand, however, one must never lose sight of the importance of paying careful attention to the exceptional conditions of human experience that give rise to exceptional decisions. Always there is room for compassionate understanding and the repentant recognition for the need of God's forgiveness in the unusual or "boundary" situation.

An aspect of suicide that is ethically quite different from terminal suicide and that needs consideration is the suicide born of despair on the part of those who are not terminally ill. Such suicide occurs with alarming frequency in men over 65. This is the second-highest risk group in the population, surpassed only by adolescents between 17 and 25. Such a statistic must make us as a society and a church consider why this is occurring. What is there about our society and our life for single and widowed men over 65 that makes life so unbearable as to call for this radical solution? Why is life not worth living for certain individuals in our society? The condemnation for suicide of this type should often be directed at the materialistic and individualistic society rather than at the individuals who take their own lives.

Does not this indicate a responsibility, particularly for the church and local congregations, to be sensitive to this age group in their communities and the threat to life that their situation poses? Are we not bound to do what is necessary to bring comfort, support, and caring to such lonely persons, as well as struggle to solve the problem with public moral policy and appropriate legislation?

The debate in these matters of death with dignity, of prolonging life or terminating the burden of suffering, usually revolves around the issue of what death is, or better, when death occurs. The medical community seems fairly well agreed now on this with the consensus of "brain death," to be considered along with the usual indicators of vital signs. But what is also involved and more difficult is the issue of what constitutes life.

Facing both these questions requires that one finally go beyond technology science and enter into the arena of values. The Christian perspective here has profound validity not only for Christians but for the larger society as well. It centers on respect for life or, better, the cherishing of life. The life that we cherish is not merely breathing air and pumping blood for three score years or more; the life we cherish is lived in community, in personal relationship under God, who gives life, with other persons and in self-awareness. Vital signs, such as brain functioning, are but the guarantors or the vehicles that make such living possible. Death and dying can take place through the destruction of the relational elements of being, just as much as through loss of physical ability to live. When we lose the capacity to be and respond in relationships, we are already dying, just as at the beginning of life, after having begun to breathe, we begin to respond and interact with mother and then others and so begin to live. Consideration of this sort can be kept in mind as one faces the dilemmas of dying.

The Christian perspective also includes the important element of awareness that the life we live on earth and in time and space does not trace the full dimensions of the life God has prepared for us. Within this perspective, when the dying process is clearly under way, one can more easily surrender life into the hands of the one who gave it. There is less need to grasp at every single additional hour or day. Pastors, by their very presence, often symbolize this hope and this perspective, which can provide support and help in these dilemmas of dying.

10

Pastoral Counseling with Elders

It will be helpful to distinguish different types of pastoral care and counseling. Most common is that which provides support, strength, and companionship in a situation that is extremely trying or burdensome. Persons who are suffering the loss of a loved one or enduring illness or experiencing great pain need support and companionship, whatever their age. Persons in crisis situations need a special type of supportive counseling as they try to hold themselves together to meet the crisis. Elders often have a special need for support as they face grief, loneliness, illness, pain, and death.

Another form of counseling that a pastor is frequently called on to provide involves self-understanding, self-exploration, self-clarification, or insight. This counseling is needed by, for example, a high school or college student weighing alternate career options. A clear understanding of the talents, skills, and interests a person has is essential at a time like that, and pastoral counseling can often be very helpful in providing it. Self-exploration and self-clarification are significant in soul care, when repentance and confession are involved. The emphasis here is on helping others to see themselves as they really are, rather than as they fantasize themselves to be or hope they might be. Counseling of this sort is not unique to any age group; it could be especially helpful in a mid-life crisis and also at retirement, when self-examination and self-exploration are called for as one reestablishes or redefines life goals. When we get rid of the stereotype that regards old age as a disease, requiring simply support and comfort, and begin to think of older people as effective, growing, searching, thinking, and feeling persons like the rest of us, then pastoral care and counseling that aids self-awareness and facilitates effective decision making will become more common.

Another form of pastoral counseling is increasingly being called for as living becomes more complex and the ethical choices that people must make are more difficult. This could be called *ethical guidance*—help toward arriving at appropriate decisions. Decision-making counseling employs many of the same skills and the same artful sense of compassion as do the other two forms. It exercises them differently, however. Usually this form of counseling is not long-term but is terminated when an appropriate decision has been made.

Since this is not a textbook specifically on pastoral counseling, we cannot venture into a detailed treatment of all these forms of pastoral care. Yet a brief sketch of the essential elements of these three forms of counseling applied to the needs of older persons may be helpful.

Supportive counseling with elders

Mary E. was a woman of some 70 years who had been living with her sister until a recent fall. She injured her back in the fall and was now in the intensive care unit of a church-related nursing home. She was visited by a young man, a student in ministry. Mary had been slowly recovering from her fall. She often talked of wanting to die. She had a good memory, vividly recalling earlier conversations with her visitor.

Visitor: I bet you thought I had forgotten about you, since I didn't stop last Wednesday.

Mary: I missed you. Can you get a chair? Pastor R. was in to see me this morning. He read Scripture and had a prayer. He doesn't like me to talk about wanting to die. He says life is a gift from God.

Visitor: It is hard to see this when you have to suffer so much, isn't it?

Mary: I've had about everything a person could have. I don't have anyone living any longer. I'm the oldest and the only one left. I'm 72. Katy [her roommate in the infirmary] is older than I am, but she doesn't look it. She had a stroke and can't talk. I have heart trouble, hardening of the arteries. (*She went on to talk about a niece and her family, then changed the subject.*) Dr. R. told me that you would be coming to visit me. I think he is disgusted with me for wanting to die.

Visitor: I don't think he is disgusted with you. It's hard for us to understand when we haven't suffered as you have. I don't think it is bad for you to think about dying. You don't need to be ashamed.

Mary: I wondered what you thought.

Visitor: It's hard for us to understand why we have to suffer, and why God doesn't let us die. In our weakness I guess we have to trust and have faith that he knows what is best.

Mary (*acquiescing*): Yes, God knows what is best.

Visitor: And when we think of heaven and the joy we will have there, our sufferings don't seem so bad.

Reading this account, we can see several points at which both pastor and visitor were not listening carefully to the feelings and concerns being expressed. When the student did hear them, he responded only at the cognitive level. But what we want to see here is the real need for support that Mary was expressing and to explore briefly what supportive counseling means in a situation like this.

In a word, supportive counseling is *experienced compassion.* It is the awareness in the person being helped that someone who cares about them is standing alongside and experiencing their hurts, their fears, and their terror, even as they are.[1]

Compassionate listening is the essence of the skill for providing support. With such listening the troubled elder is able to express outwardly the fears, the hurts, the sense of loneliness and worthlessness that has been held inside for fear no one would understand. Providing support means offering a setting where one's worst fears and deepest feelings can be expressed and understood without censure. This is supportive, because as the person verbalizes these worst fears, they are externalized—released, as it were, from the troubled mind—to be examined for their meaning and significance. The "worst case scenario" is exposed to the light of day, and in that light there is the possibility for a new perspective on it, and for beginning to determine what action, if any, can be taken to brace oneself for or ward off what may come.

Supportive counseling, furthermore, delivers strength and courage to the one being helped. Early in the history of modern psychotherapy, some of the pioneers spoke of the process as the "lending of the ego"; the counselor, presumably stronger at the moment (at least not paralyzed by fears, anxieties, doubts, and pain) "lends" his or her ego to the person temporarily weakened by the burdens of living. Sharing one's ego as caregiver does not necessarily mean giving advice or direction to the person being helped, however. On some occasions this may be necessary, but it tends to be rarer than we helpers usually think.

Given this kind of support, the person in counseling may well be able to "turn the corner," and just a small turn of the corner may be all that is needed to set things right again. In the interview above, the pastoral visitor offered such support with the comment, "It's hard for us to understand why we have to suffer, and why God doesn't let us die." In the simple verbalizing of the "doubting faith" and by the use of "we" language, the pastor was giving support, standing by with a symbolic hand on the shoulder of Mary, who was trying to face death.

Supportive care, it should be clear, is not giving hasty or even false reassurance. The novice, or the person who really doesn't want to expose him or herself to the real pain and struggle, may offer premature reassurance: "Mary, don't worry about how the doctor feels. Before too long he'll have you right as rain. You just concentrate on getting well." Such a response attempts to cheer up Mary by denying what she is struggling with. In effect it is saying, "If you don't worry about it, it will go away." In addition, such a statement is partially false. The pastor has no evidence whatsoever that Mary will be "right as rain." In fact, all the evidence points in the opposite direction, and Mary knows it. For a pastor to offer glib reassurance would say to Mary, "I can't really talk to the pastor; he doesn't understand." Support means facing the realities along with the suffering person, usually at the pace he or she is able to take. It means providing strength so that the person who is unwilling to face the realities may have the companionship and the strength to do so.

Counseling for self-understanding with elders

When I began the study of pastoral counseling some 30 years ago, it was believed that "insight counseling," or counseling for personality change or clarification, was relatively useless for people over 55. That view is now outmoded. Not only can we "teach an old dog new tricks," but we can help "old dogs" understand themselves and use themselves more effectively. Insight or self-clarification counseling, however, generally calls for specialized skills and more time than is available to a parish pastor. Consequently most counseling of this type is referred to specialists. But in order to make an effective referral, a pastor needs to be aware that this sort of growth experience is what a person needs and is ready for, and in discovering this the pastor engages, at a preliminary level, in self-exploration with older parishioners.

An alternate form of insight counseling is spiritual guidance or spiritual direction, in which personal behavior, attitudes, motives, and sensibilities are explored with the dual intention of better self-understanding as well as healthier spiritual life. Counseling of this sort may be particularly desirable for older persons.

If it is true, as Erikson, Levinson, Neugarten, and others have contended, that persons are always growing, developing, and changing, then there is always a need for and the potential for increased self-understanding and spiritual direction.

In the case noted above, Mary exhibited some need for understanding her own feelings and motives more clearly when she expressed concern that the pastor was disgusted at her for wanting to die. She might have been expressing her own disgust at this attitude, and she may also have been wondering what made her feel so discouraged about life. Clearly she was wondering whether it was truly bad to have such thoughts. All these issues are in the province of this type of counseling and are appropriate for a pastor to pursue, so long as the level of concern remains with conscious, reasonably contemporary, issues.

In another interview, which took place in a nursing home, a middle-old person, age 69, who was suffering some emotional reactions as the result of the untimely death of her husband, confided in the pastoral visitor:

> I just don't like it here. I have never lived in this town. I lived all my life in Greenville, and after my husband died recently, I decided to break up housekeeping. I didn't know where to go. I suppose I could have set up an apartment somewhere, but I didn't know how my health would hold up. And then I had all that trouble about those pressures.
>
> You see, my husband was sick for a very long time. It was just like three years taken right out of my life. You're young and can't understand just what I mean, but we had lived and worked hard for the time we could retire and just as soon as he retired he got sick. I tell you it was really hard.

Several issues for self-clarification, insight, and emotional growth are evident here. She needed some help in dealing with her grief and some understanding of how her unresolved grief was affecting her right then. She needed to express the anger she felt for having gotten a "raw deal," and she could have been helped to deal with her sense of meaning and purpose in life, either to ratify her decision to be where she was or to make a new decision. All of this is a form of spiritual guidance and self-awareness. But to provide this would take considerable time and much skill in dealing with the issues of which she was aware and helping her to recognize some of her unconscious conflicts. Often a collaborative relationship with a psychiatrist or psychotherapist who deals with the deeper issues is helpful.

I can see a real need for this type of pastoral counseling for marriages of older persons. It is becoming increasingly evident that marriages of 25, 30, and 40 years duration often need some help. Much of this is help in the arenas of self-understanding and understanding each other.

Professional psychotherapists and specialists in pastoral counseling usually recommend that parish pastors be very cautious about becoming involved in "self-awareness counseling" that extends beyond six sessions, partly because longer segments of time in counseling generate a more intense relationship. One helpful suggestion from Pastor Barry Estadt is that counseling of this sort be considered in the light of the liturgical calendar.[2] The pastor and the parishioner agree to meet for an hour a week for reflection during the Advent or Lenten season. This puts a clear limit on the relationship and allows for the possibility for further negotiation of extensions or, perhaps more advisable, consideration of referral to a specialist.[3]

Crisis counseling with elders

Crisis care is called for whenever a person's or a family's normal equilibrium or sense of balance in dealing with life's problems becomes disrupted, or when people feel that the magnitude of a problem overwhelms their resources. Crises may be *developmental*, as we have seen from our study of developmental issues in aging. Retirement is such a crisis. Crises may also be *situational*, as in the instance of a person retiring and then suddenly discovering that the stocks and bonds that were to be retirement income have lost their value. Crises of illness, a terminal diagnosis, and an unexpected death in the family are all situational.

The mode for dealing with crises is an important part of a parish pastor's equipment for ministry. Fortunately, because crisis intervention is so common in ministry, most pastors have received training in this area. There are also many excellent teaching resources available in books and in workshops conducted by area mental-health centers, pastoral counseling centers, and teaching chaplains.[4]

In a hospital interview with the wife of a man in his late 50s who was suffering from the results of a heart attack, we can see the dimensions of crisis and some of the means for crisis care.

Margaret: I've been here day after day for eight weeks, and I don't live close to the hospital, either. Sometimes I take the bus or sometimes I walk.

Pastor: You just want to make sure you are close to Jim.

Margaret: Oh, yes. I don't want to be gone too long. My children think I'm crazy. My son, he's 16, thinks it is stupid to spend

day after day with someone who cannot even talk to you.
But he does not understand. They do not even help at home.
They expect me to be home to cook and clean for them.

Pastor: They would like things to be back to normal again.

Margaret: Yes, but they cannot be that way again. We were close,
so close. They thought that Jim could be released this week.
But then on Sunday everything changed. He was doing so
well that he was walking around the floor. When he came
back here, he got into bed and asked me to give him a sponge
bath. So I took off the top of his pajamas and was sponging
him down when he started to shake. I thought it was because
the water was too cold. So I stopped bathing him and put
the cloth on his forehead. No sooner had I done that when
his eyes rolled back into his head and he stopped breathing.
After that, all I remember was running out to the nurses'
desk screaming. The nurses told me I went crazy. They said
I started running and screaming all over the place, and I
finally collapsed in the hall. I just fainted dead away. But I
don't remember any of that.

Pastor: I can't imagine what that would feel like. It must have
been terrifying.

Margaret: You don't know how scared you can be until it's someone you love. I'm not like that, normally. My friends call me
a rock, but Sunday I just went to pieces.

Pastor: Of course you felt you went to pieces. You thought you
had just seen your husband die.

Margaret: Yes, I thought I had lost him. I thought he was gone,
but—(*her voice trails off*).

Pastor: But you are still concerned about how you acted and
what the nurses will be thinking about you.

Margaret: I don't know what they think about me, but I believe,
you know. (*Looking the visitor straight in the eye.*) I do have
faith. I trust in God. He has done so many good things for
us.

Pastor: I don't doubt that you believe in God, but just because we believe does not mean that we are not afraid.

Margaret: You are so right on that one! I've never been so scared in all my whole life.

Pastor: That's natural. Having faith in God doesn't mean we won't be afraid. In fact, God is aware of our fear. He knows we're scared. The first thing he normally says to anyone in the Bible when he comes to them is, "Fear not." He says that to reassure us even as he comes to us. Our fear does not keep him away.

Here we see all three of the elements of a crisis intertwined. The sudden heart attack was a real threat to Margaret that she would lose a loved lifelong companion. Now contemplating his life and the continuing possibility of his death, she was also coming to terms with loss, yet she saw it to be a challenge to come to terms with this loss in her faith-life. She wanted to come through this crisis with her faith in God strengthened and with her family intact.

Often what makes a crisis is not only the event that is felt as threat or loss or challenge, but the *perception* of the event. Religious faith is exceedingly important in this regard. It would have been an even greater crisis for Margaret if she had perceived the heart attack and threatened loss of her husband as a sign of God's displeasure with her; she would then have been threatened not only with the loss of love and support from her husband, but with the loss of God's support as well.

Crisis counseling attempts to right the balance of resources, threat, and perception—to give a person a sense of being able to cope with the crisis. Sometimes this involves helping the person use an alternate set of coping mechanisms or ways of dealing with the crisis, especially when the customary ones don't work.

Pastor Howard Stone has devised a simple method for dealing with crises that involves three major signs or processes (*Crisis Counseling*, Fortress, 1976). First, establish contact with the crisis-stricken person; provide a relationship of compassion and support. Second, break up the crisis event into manageable pieces—"divide and conquer." Third, help the crisis victim focus on one or another of these pieces that can be dealt with, and help him or her do so with confidence and effectiveness. This builds further confidence so that new coping mechanisms can be put in place of the habitual ones that no longer work. All along, a pastor helps the person gain a more realistic and constructive perception of the meaning of the crisis event. This involves helping the person to see the crisis sequence in the faith that God walks through the crisis with us, suffers it with us, and shares with us his victory, ultimately over death itself.

One of the forms of crisis that occurs with alarming frequency in ministry to older persons is attempted suicide. For the person contemplating suicide, life no longer feels either worth living or bearable; death seems the more attractive alternative. Since all of us constantly live in the delicate balance between cherishing life and feeling the seductive pull of death, dealing with a suicidal person affects this delicate balance within the helping person as well. We easily become anxious, and in our own need to feel safer we are tempted to maneuver the troubled person into artificial resolutions of the crisis. We may therefore fail to hear or see the signals the troubled person is sending.

The Los Angeles Suicide Prevention Center has developed a set of characteristics by which a pastor or family member can determine how likely a suicide attempt might be. Some of the more important variables are:

Age and Sex: Men over 55 are in the highest danger bracket.

Symptoms: Suicide risk is higher if a person is severely depressed, is feeling hopeless or helpless, is suffering extreme exhaustion, or is alcoholic or otherwise drug-dependent.

Stressor: Suicide is more likely if the symptoms (of illness, disability, or even suicide attempts) are chronic rather than acute.

Suicidal Plan: The more organized, detailed, and lethal a plan for suicide, the more likely it is that a person intends to implement it. If a person threatens to get a gun or to save up sleeping pills, the threat of suicide is less imminent than if the person has a gun or already has saved up enough pills for a lethal dose.

Emotional Resources: If a person has no source of support from family, friends, or work colleagues, there is more danger of suicide than if there is available family, church, clergy, and friendship support.

Prior Attempts: The likelihood of suicide is greater if there have been prior attempts. In this connection, one should always take seriously talk about suicide. It is not true that people who talk about suicide won't do it.

Medical Status: Suicide potential is higher if the person is suffering from a long-term, debilitating illness.

Communication Outlets: The more outlets a person has for communicating feelings of guilt, anger, fear, shame, pain, and blame, the less potential for suicide.

Reaction of Significant Loved Ones: Suicide potential is higher if significant loved ones will blame or reject the person for the suicide. Often a motive for suicide is not self-destruction but, indirectly, the destruction of others.

Pastoral procedure in the crisis of attempted suicide must be as immediate as possible and should strike a balance between detached calm and panic. Rachel Callahan of the Loyola Pastoral Counseling Service suggests these additional measures for dealing with the suicidal person.[5] Keep the person talking as a way of verbally discharging the despair, anger, and pain that provide impetus for the suicide. A supportive relationship is a necessary part of pastoral intervention. Mobilization of an effective community or familial support network with much human contact with the suicidal person is most helpful. A basic goal of suicide counseling is to enlarge the person's sense of alternatives so that there are other ways out than death. Personal contact and concern, as well as familial concern, help to enlarge the person's sense of self-worth. A person who is suicidal should never be left alone until the period of danger and despair are past. Ultimately, pastoral care for suicidal persons involves dealing with the family as well as with the person who is threatening this action.

A pastor has a very special role and power in crisis intervention counseling. He or she is a "sacramental person" who embodies the transcendent, ultimate, compassionate care of God in all of life. This embodiment carries with it a great deal of symbolic power which can work toward healing and life, or despair and death, depending on the religious experience and perspective of the person being helped. A pastor is one of the most accessible helping persons in our society. A pastor communicates the ultimate care and concern of God, the grace and blessing of God, in all of the critical developmental passages of life, birth, maturity, marriage, vocation, and death. A pastor can facilitate the almost immediate networking of support systems for the crisis-invaded person, calling on family, congregation, community, and society for necessary help. Particularly for older persons who still have remnants of a well-developed heritage of faith, a pastor is a first line of defense in crisis.

Counseling for decision and action with elders

This type of counseling is probably called for more often than most pastors or helping persons make use of it. In so many situations in life after 65, important decisions have to be made, and the person who is confronted with the decision really needs and welcomes some help in the process.[6] All too often, however, the persons around the elder assume that the best help they can give is to take over the decision-making process. Is it possible that we think that the presence of severe arthritis, gout, heart disease, advanced forms of cancer, or whatever the illness may be, automatically also renders a person incapable of thinking, feeling or deciding? It certainly seems so in the instance of Frank J., an elderly widower of 86 who has heart disease and is troubled with failing vision and hearing. The pastor was visiting with him in a nursing home and he described his life there:

Frank: Oh, it's nice and all that, but what do you have to do but get up, eat, go back to your room, watch TV, eat again, go back to the room again, eat, and go to bed?

Pastor: I guess that would get kind of monotonous after a while.

Frank: Yes. You know, I don't even know why I'm here. I've got three daughters. One lives in this little town near here. Before I came here, she took pretty good care of me, but her husband is not well either, so when he traveled, she had to go along with him and they didn't want to leave me in the house by myself. Then I have another daughter down in Florida. I was with her for 11 months, but sometimes she would be gone for maybe a week or more and didn't want to leave me alone either. So I guess the three of them put their heads together, and the first thing I know, I'm in here.

Frank then went on to describe his life before coming to the home. He liked to walk out in the open spaces. For 14 years he had lived by himself.

Frank: I lived by myself and did all my own housework, cooking and cleaning, etc. Of course, I didn't keep it clean like a woman, but I got along pretty well. I lived right next to a golf course and I used to get my clubs and play practically all day long. Well, that went on pretty good until my daughter wanted me to come and live with her. But I liked to get out and walk, and there isn't much of that here.

It is quite likely that Frank's daughters and sons-in-law were deeply concerned about his safety while living alone. Their concern about his capability to care for himself was no doubt well founded. His heart problems and failing vision and hearing quite possibly made continued living alone somewhat dangerous. Yet in listening to him one has the feeling that he would have liked to try to continue to manage, and could have, with some occasional help in housekeeping or meals or some other arrangements. One gets the sense that he wasn't allowed to consider any of these options or become a part of the decision for his further life. In a situation like this, counseling for decision making would have been most helpful for Frank and also for the members of his family.

Often the whole family must be involved in the process leading to a decision for the life-style of an elder.[7] Like all other forms of counseling, this, too, depends a great deal on the primary resource of a compassionate, trusting relationship between the counselor and those who must make decisions. Respect for the person is necessary. Each of us is a child of God, created in the image of God, no matter how old, infirm, ill, irritating, or demanding we might be. Respect believes that each person would like to do the best he or she can do, and is still able to make decisions or at least be party to decisions. To arbitrarily take away another's ability to decide—to ignore his or her *right* to decide—is to show the ultimate disrespect.

When compassionate listening, respect, and concern are present, persons we are working with feel able to trust us, to trust that we do indeed have their best interests at heart. We can be trusted to give them help in a way that is not demeaning. The trust level in a counseling relationship moves in both directions, from the counselor to the counselee, and from the counselee to the counselor. When such trust is present, the fear that one's power to decide will arbitrarily be taken away is minimized. Instead, one gains additional strength to see alternatives clearly and have the courage to decide.

Defining the problems

After this basic relationship of trust has been established, the next step is to define the problem. This step is deceptive. It seems so simple for the counselor standing on the outside of another's life looking in, but to the person in the middle of the muddle, it is not simple at all. The important feature of this step is that the problem must be defined *by the person in the muddle,* not the family or a counselor. All of us know how irritating it is to have someone say to us, after we have expressed our frustration or fears, "Well, the trouble with you is. . . . " or "What you ought to do is. . . . " The older person feels this all the more because it is another form of infantilizing or patronizing, of making the older person feel useless and incompetent.

Defining, or putting boundaries around the problem, is a matter of careful listening. One listens not only for feelings, opinions, and attitudes, but also for factual or historical content—what is happening in the life of the person being counseled. It is this combination of happenings and feelings that must be carefully blended by the person and the pastor before the problem can be outlined. The following example may help to make clearer what is involved here.

Older Person: I received a telegram this morning from my mother. She said dad is dying. The doctors believe he will live only a few days longer. My dad and I were never close. We haven't spoken to each other in years. I guess both of us are pretty stubborn. Now that he's dying, I feel awful. I think I care about him more than I ever realized. I don't want him to die with things the way they are between us.

The feelings being expressed: a mixture of shock, sadness, regret, guilt, uncertainty or confusion, and deep uneasiness.

The content of what is happening: a telegram informing her that her father is dying. She and her father are not on good terms. She wants to change the alienated relationship.

At least three problems can be defined: First, should she go immediately to her father's bedside even though they are estranged? Second, should she do something to repair the relationship before she goes home? Third, how can she best give support and comfort to her mother?

The important thing here is to determine which of the several problems is most important to the person involved. Often a pastor can be most helpful by identifying the several problems present, as in the above example. Usually the person seeing them spelled out will be motivated to select those that are most pressing. Clarifying the various issues in this way is also helpful in another sense: it breaks up what seems to be an insurmountable problem into manageable pieces.

Setting goals

This leads then to the next step, goal setting, which rather naturally grows out of defining the problems. One of the problems that is important to the older person is selected, and the collaborating pair—pastor and elder parishioner—begin to explore ways of dealing with the problem. It is important to select a problem that has some reasonable chance of solution. It is only common sense to address the problem that can be solved and leave that which cannot. The skill is in knowing the difference.

Another way of looking at this is to determine with clarity what is the elder's problem and what is another's problem. In the vignette above, the troubled daughter cannot change her father's attitude toward her, but she can change her attitude toward her father. How she feels about him is her problem; how he feels about her is his problem. Recognizing which problems belong to us and which are another's is an important issue in problem-solving counseling. Often here the pastor can once again be helpful in the clarifying process.

Setting goals is simply a matter of considering the steps that might be taken to change things. In doing this, careful attention should be given to the feelings surrounding the problem. In the situation given, we need to consider whether a sudden visit to this woman's father would only further upset him, given his precarious physical condition. How will she feel if she does not go to visit him and he dies? Will the visit be unbearably anxiety-provoking for the daughter? What will she say to her father? How will she respond to his possible response? The exploration of all these issues can be helpful in choosing the most appropriate action.

Exploring alternatives

Arriving at a solution or a course of action for a given problem always involves examining the various alternatives. There is hardly ever only one "right" way to proceed. In the situation of the estranged daughter, several alternatives appear possible, assuming that the collaborating pair have decided that the primary goal is to do something to alter the estranged relationship. The daughter is to make some move of reconciliation toward her father. What shall that move be? Several alternatives appear: she could get on a plane and go immediately to her father's bedside. What should she say? If she is ready to forgive and be forgiven, she can express this to him, if his physical condition warrants. Or she might write a letter of reconciliation before her visit. She might telephone him, assuming he is able to speak to her.

Each of these alternatives should be explored carefully as to their possibility and potential outcome. In an instance such as this one, the pastor ought to give special attention to the attitudes and feelings of the daughter. For example, if she decides to write a letter of reconciliation, is she truly forgiving, or is she being driven only by fear that he will die and she will feel guilty? Is she ready to examine her own contribution to the estrangement? This becomes spiritual guidance.

A pastor can be especially helpful in identifying alternatives for action, but care must be exercised to suggest more than one alternative. To suggest only one alternative will come across as, "That is what the pastor thinks I should do." The decision then becomes the pastor's and not the parishioner's. It is wise, therefore, to suggest at least two, and preferably three, alternatives, even though one or the other of them seems more desirable to the pastor. Sometimes it is even helpful to suggest alternatives that are a bit far out, either in terms of feasibility or morality, as a stimulus to get the parishioner thinking.

The next step is the exploration of the feasibility or wisdom of each of the alternatives. Alternative courses of action are to be explored not only as to their possibility, wisdom, and morality, but as to their consequences. Will the proposed course of action create further damage to the relationship, or will it be likely to lead to reconciliation? Both positive and negative consequences are to be explored, the positive and negative effects of the action on both parties in the relationship.

It is at this point of selecting alternative courses for action by examining their consequences that a pastor can best give the kind of spiritual and ethical guidance that is so often necessary in decisions about human relationships. When introduced at this point, ethical or moral concerns do not carry the heavy "you ought to" freight that they would if such suggestions were made when identifying the problem. As in so much of careful pastoral care, timing is important.

Just as important as achieving reconciliation is the maintenance of personal integrity—for both father and daughter. If the daughter is led to an apology—or to repentance—under some sort of coercion, then the loss of her own integrity and the subsequent effect on the relationship are to be considered.

Here important theological issues come to the fore: the matters of judgment and grace. If daughter and father are to be reconciled by forgiving each other, then to some degree the attitudes, behavior, and feelings that have been damaging to each other must be recognized. The daughter must recognize the actions or sins committed by her father against her. In the situation we are thinking of, it may not be wise to surface these in conversation directly with her father, but surely they would be appropriate in conversation with the pastor, with her mother, or in prayer to God. Forgiveness is never just a vague blanket pardon, but is always directed to actions destructive to our relationships with others and with God. The effect of forgiveness on those forgiven is that the person is forgiven along with the actions which are forgiven.

Making the decision and acting on it

Now we are ready for the final step—making the decision and carrying it out. The pastoral role is primarily to give support and encouragement. Support may take the form first of confirming the decision, making sure that it is genuine and that it feels comfortable to the person. Further support might then be given by "walking through" the decision and the subsequent action. In the situation we have been considering, this might take the following form.

Pastor: Now tell me once again what you have decided and how you feel about this decision.

Daughter: Well, I think it is very important that my dad and I be reconciled before his death. I know I'll never forgive myself if I don't at least try. I'm very comfortable with our conclusion that I should write a brief letter that mother can perhaps read to him. I will prepare then to take a plane home as soon as they have received the letter. I can check that out by telephone.

Pastor: And have you thought through what you will write in the letter?

Daughter: Yes, I want to tell him how much our estrangement over the past several years has been lonely for me, and I'm sure for him, too. I'll mention what it was that particularly put me off in his actions, but I want to tell him that while this hurt me, I do want to put it behind us and I forgive him for this. But most of all, I want to tell him that I am sorry for the way I have hurt him, particularly for that time when—

Pastor: Writing that all out will bring some healing to you then, too?

Daughter: Yes, I'm sure it will. I feel better about my dad already just from talking about it. I'm ready to do what should be done.

This final phase of the pastoral counseling in a situation of this sort is what we might call simply follow-up. The pastor might do this by determining whether the letter was written, what the writer's reaction was, and if possible, what the receiver's action was, and what next steps are now indicated. It may well be that unforeseen consequences generate new problems that call for different actions, so the process of counseling for a decision might begin all over again.

Pastoral conversation with the confused elder

One of the ministries of greatest frustration is conversation with the confused elder who is suffering from various degrees of senile dementia with resulting loss of clear perception of reality. Conversation with the confused person requires a high degree of ingenuity, patience, sensitivity, and imagination. The most helpful counsel I have found for ministry in this difficult situation is an article by Dr. Albert Meiburg.[8]

Dr. Meiburg suggests three basic strategies in conversation with the confused elder: (1) those that help to focus the person's attention on the visit; (2) those that help to foster the person's orientation to reality; and (3) those that strive to find meaning in the person's expression and experiences.

One of the aspects of confusion with elders of this type is their difficulty in centering their attention for any length of time. Therefore, all efforts by the pastor to control extraneous distractions—simplifying the environment or simplifying one's speech—will make it easier for the elder to keep attention centered on the conversation. Thus a conversation with the person in a wheelchair sitting in a busy hallway will be much more difficult than if the elder were moved to a quiet, simple room. Dr. Meiburg stresses that removing the person from distracting public gaze is usually helpful. Even confused persons who seem not to know what's going on should have their privacy respected.

The visitor should also pay special attention to sensory impairments of various kinds; if the person normally wears glasses, it would be helpful if he or she is encouraged to wear them during the visit so that important eye contact can be enhanced. Likewise with hearing aids; often elders do not wear them regularly because they are irritating. It would be easier for the person to wear the aid in a quiet room where there are fewer distracting noises. As noted earlier, give careful attention to pitch and intensity of your voice when speaking. These suggestions seem obvious and therefore they are often overlooked.

More complicated than simple hearing difficulty is the disorder known as *aphasia* resulting from stroke or brain disorder. The problem is not so much with hearing, as it is with the ability to "compute" what is heard or what one wishes to say. Slowing down the pace of the conversation is often helpful. As one elder put it, according to Dr. Meiburg, "I hear all right, but, you see, I hear more slowly since my stroke." And usually such persons also speak more slowly as well. In one study of 50 people who recovered from aphasia following stroke, M. Skelly found that all of them were able to understand what was said to them much sooner than they were able to respond. Their complaint was, "Nobody talked *to* me, only *about* me."[9]

Because of the isolation of illness and institutionalization, older persons want desperately to communicate and so want to please the one who visits. As a result they may be reluctant to admit that they don't understand and so will respond yes to all questions without always meaning yes. Sometimes visitors do the same with aphasic people who have difficulty speaking; to avoid embarrassing them we say "I understand" when we really don't. It would be better to admit that we do not understand; this will also make it easier for them to admit they do not always understand or have difficulty in framing words and sentences.

In instances where spoken communication is extremely difficult, sensitive attention to nonverbal communication can be useful. "I'm not sure what you want, but I can see that you are uncomfortable. Is something wrong with your bed?" Or, "It must be awfully frustrating to want to say something and not be able to get it out." Sometimes one can assist the person to get the word out that they are struggling with, but be careful not to cross the fine line of putting words in the person's mouth. As Meiburg observes, "For the aphasic person to sense that his or her efforts are being taken seriously, and that at least some parts of the message are getting through is a source of great encouragement."

One form of communication that is useful is physical touch. In pastoral visiting touching should usually be limited to the handclasp or the "hand of blessing." One nurse described a farmer who could not be interested in eating because in his fantasies he was preoccupied with directing his farmhands. She found that if she took him by the hand, she gained his attention, so she held his hand while feeding him.

Focusing orientation to reality is aided by the following guidelines suggested by Meiburg.

1. Call the person by name at the beginning of the visit and do not hesitate to use it frequently during the visit. It communicates respect and enhances dignity to call an older person by Mr. or Mrs., or by their professional title if they have one. Intimacy is not automatically communicated nor gained by indiscriminate use of first names.

2. Always introduce yourself by name at the beginning of the conversation, unless it is perfectly clear that you are recognized. It might help, then, to ask the person to say your name.

3. Help orient the person to the time of day and the day of the week. A casual reference to the time of day is helpful. Symbolic references and images of the church year are liturgically appropriate and helpful in orienting the person.

4. Encourage continued contact with the outside world through use of the parish newsletter, Sunday bulletin, daily newspaper, denominational periodicals, and the telephone.

5. Simplify the conversation and pace it appropriately to the person's orientation and abilities.

6. In the conversation search for areas and periods of life in which the person functions effectively. It may well be that the only avenue for communication with an elderly woman is

through her role as mother, talking about her children. With a professional person that might occur in talk about his or her profession.

7. It is best to avoid trying to respond to delusions or hallucinations. It is better to continue to stress the present reality. "Neither argument about delusional content nor confirmation ('tell me more about your airplane trip yesterday') seem to be helpful," observes Meiburg. If delusions persist and some response is called for, basic empathy is most useful.

Perhaps the most difficult task with the confused older person is simply to understand what they mean by what they are saying. As one hears the elaborate delusion spelled out or tries to follow the intricacies of the hallucination, one wonders, "What is the person experiencing or feeling in all of this?" Like the psychiatrist, the minister struggles to discover the basic meaning to the person hidden within the seeming nonsense of disordered thought. To get at this it is helpful to appreciate what dementia does to the basic thought process. Essentially it reduces the ability to do abstract thinking: thought processes become more concrete, and logical thinking is replaced with feeling. Secondly, ideas may be expressed by their opposites; opposing ideas are put side by side. Third, the concepts of conditionality and possibility are missing; ambiguity is not understood or tolerated. Fourth, there is a limited time sense. Fifth, the concept of self-accountability is lost or minimized. Finally, there is primary reliance on the pleasure principle and universal feelings remain available. That is, the person's total range of feelings clamor for expression or satisfaction. The thinking of the severely confused person resembles what we experience in our own dreams, or when we are totally governed by impulses such as joy, rage, or love.

Meiburg cautions us to bear in mind that "although the communications of a confused person may be logically incongruous, on a feeling level there is a basis of reality." Our task is to discern and respond to this reality. Feelings generated by a particular person encountered years ago may be easily transferred to the present situation; an argument with father, from childhood, may become an argument with the pastor because of the similarity of roles and the feelings that role generates. Dr. Adrian Verwoerdt reports an illustration of this process.

> A 78-year-old woman's first statement to me was "your wife has died." There were several levels of meaning to this; at the moment of getting acquainted, the relevant idea was that if my wife was dead, we would be "available" for each other—and that for this to be on her mind, she probably liked me; somebody cared for her. She provided further evidence of this, saying: "And she over here (the nurse) is your daughter." Through this concrete transference, she expressed a specific feeling; that it was like a family here, that she felt "at home."[10]

To this, an appropriate empathic response might be, "It feels like a family here with the three of us." Later in the interview, Dr. Verwoerdt reports she stated:

> "Now you and I are married"—ideas of permanence and closeness are expressed through the concept of marriage. Proceeding along her line of thought I asked if she was going to be in a family way. "Oh, yes, we'll have children, but not now, in a few years. . . . " In other words, the closeness between us will not end for quite a while.

One listens for the fundamental symbols or metaphors the person is using and then determines what meaning those symbols might have for the person speaking. Thus, marriage as a fundamental symbol communicates love, caring, permanency; the family (doctor, person, nurse) symbolizes caring, love, permanency, and absence of loneliness. The sexual symbolism communicates something of the depth of love and the feeling of intimacy.

One cannot effectively decode these symbols until one knows the person and his or her life story quite well. Here the pastor or parish visitor who has known the elder for an extended period of time is at a distinct advantage, both as regards the trust level as well as awareness of what the symbols might mean.

The importance of understanding the symbolic language of the confused elder works also in reverse, because then the skillful pastor can also make use of similar symbols in communicating back to the confused person. Here the rich symbolic language of Scripture can be particularly helpful, especially that of the Old Testament, notably the Psalms. A similar use of symbols occurs in the Psalms; recall the use of "father" or "mother" or "children." These symbols will reach the confused person when abstractions and ideas cannot.

Pastoral conversation, then, is possible with confused elders. It takes great patience, compassionate concern, imaginative sensitivity, and perseverance. And it is truly rewarding for the older person whose confusion may be lessened by such ministry. The isolation of the confused state of mind will be reduced, and there will be a sense that the everlasting Father has not forgotten them.

11

Family Counseling with Elders

In almost all instances a pastor has not only a particular older person to work with, but the family as well. In spite of the stereotypes, most older people do have continued, regular contact with their families. Consequently, growing old and the problems of aging are not only individual issues, but family concerns. Frequently the family needs as much pastoral attention as does the older person.

Seeing the family as a system

"Systems theory" or the "family system" has emerged as a most helpful approach to counseling. Developed first in response to troubled children and adolescents by pioneers such as Virginia Satir, it is now becoming an increasingly helpful perspective in ministry to older persons.[1] Its first principle is that family is not just a collection of individuals, but an organism, a body. Bible students will recall Paul's analogy of the church as the "body of Christ" and his detailing of interaction of this body (cf. 1 Corinthians 12). A family is such a body. Each member interacts with others, ideally for the benefit of the whole.

A further principle is that what affects one member of the body affects everyone, and what affects the total body affects each member, albeit differently. Each family "system" develops its own way to deal with information and its environment (sometimes called *input*) and in its own way produces a response (*output*). This process of dealing with the environment and responding develops a system of "family rules" by which the family maintains a certain equilibrium (sometimes called *homeostasis*). When events occur that upset this equilibrium, the family may feel itself to be in a crisis situation. The balance is disturbed when the family does not feel it has adequate resources with which to cope with the difficult situation, such as a sudden death or the heart attack of a grandmother who has been living with the family.

In such crisis situations, what the family often does is to use the procedure of "scapegoating," laying the burden of responsibility or blame on one or another member. So one member of the family may be designated as the "sick" one upon whom the family can lavish both care and affection, as well as responsibility for the family's difficulties. In systems counseling such a person is the "identified patient." Frequently this identified patient is put forward as the one needing help, and the naive counselor or pastor might be led to lavish all attention and therapy on this individual, without taking the rest of the family into account. Often this is just what the family wants, because if the whole family gets involved, it will upset the equilibrium or life-style of the family. This is frequently perceived as being too uncomfortable. Thus the grandmother who gets a heart attack may immediately be placed in a hospital and later in a nursing home, so that the remainder of the family can go about their usual life-style.

The case of Mrs. C. illustrates the importance of seeing the family as a system in which the elder is an important part.[2] Mrs. C., who was 80, was admitted to a skilled nursing facility two months prior to the events here reported. Four months before this her husband had died in bed, beside her. She didn't discover that he was dead until she tried to wake him up in the morning. After the death Mrs. C. went to live with her sister, who was in her 70s. While she was living with her sister, Mrs. C. had a cataract operation. Less than a week after Mrs. C. returned from the hospital, her sister died. She still had her eyes bandaged when she discovered that her sister was dead. After shouting for her sister to wake up, she crawled over to her bed and found her cold to the touch. She started to scream. Neighbors called the police, who took her to the emergency room. The hospital kept her for a day to sedate her. Then, because of costs, her son tried to find other places where she could get care and finally placed her in a nursing home. Since she had been there, her cataracts had healed nicely, but otherwise, according to the rest home staff, "she was just a mess." Even when heavily medicated, all she did was scream and moan and cry. She was incontinent and refused the bedpan.

One of the nurses commented to the counselor who asked about signs of brain damage or stroke or paralysis, "I haven't noticed anything . . . but just because they don't show any physical signs doesn't mean anything. . . . She's obviously senile. What difference does it make whether or not she had a stroke or her brain is just shriveling from old age?"

Upon receiving this information, the counselor made plans to talk to her son. The staff of the hospital had been having some difficulty handling his complaints about their care of his mother. One staff member noted, "I think he's feeling guilty she isn't living at home with him. Besides, whenever situations are hopeless, relatives pick one small thing and make a big deal of it. That way they feel they're doing something." Indeed, this is often the case and is one of the dynamics that the pastor should always be alert for.

The counselor was able to see Mr. C. one day when he came in to visit his mother. She commented, "I was watching you when your mother asked you to bring your father in to visit. I could see on your face how painful that experience was for you. I wish there were something I could do."

Mr. C.:   It is discouraging. She was doing so well until her sister died. It was just too much for her. I brought her here because she needed someone to watch her and to provide medical care. But ever since she's been here she's been going downhill. I'd like to take her home, but they tell me her condition is hopeless, and I'm not in a position to put my wife and teenage kids through this kind of an ordeal.

The counselor then inquired about the progress his mother had made shortly after her husband's death.

Mr. C.:   Mother took dad's death quite hard, but after a month
she began to get back on her feet. She decided that if she
didn't have Dad to read the paper for her . . . she would
have to get her cataracts removed so she could read it herself.
. . . My mother was quite a determined woman. The cataract
surgery went well, but the healing process took a bit longer
than expected. Mother is 88 and her younger sister was only
78. Her death, and finding her the way she did, was a terrible
shock.

He then went on to explain that his mother was heavily sedated
after this shock, and that it was the ophthalmologist's guess that
the shock caused a small stroke which affected her thinking and
reasoning.

The role of counselors or pastors is somewhat ambiguous in
the family system. They are a part of it and yet not a part of it.
In Harry Stack Sullivan's term, they are "participant observers."

It is most helpful for the pastor to maintain this kind of a
position in the family system, in order to be able to gain the most
accurate perception of what is going on and in order to avoid
arousing the antagonism of any of the other members of the
system, which might hamper a resolution. The position of pastors
in the family system is much the same as in marriage conflict
counseling. They must avoid "taking sides," because to do so
simply polarizes positions and makes them more rigid and less
susceptible to change. It is not an easy position to maintain, but
it is important that both counselor and pastor do not quickly
crusade for premature or uninformed change.

A counselor also needs to be concerned about the "family
rules" that govern a family system. These are quite complex and
we cannot take the time here to analyze them fully, but it is
important to note two interacting systems of rules. First there
are the rules of the institutional portion of the system; for example, one of the cardinal principles of a hospital is "don't disturb—or challenge—the doctor." Another is that "patients should
not be noisy or disruptive." In order to bring this about, there
is collaboration, the second system of rules; for example, medication that makes patients manageable. In the C. family, one
rule seems to be "determination, perseverance at all costs," a

result of Mrs. C.'s own determination. To bring about change, these rules may need to be modified in the most beneficial way. Not only the original, usually benevolent, intent of family rules must be considered, but also the actual *effect* of the rules in a given situation. If this is destructive or hampering growth or cure, then modifications or relaxing of rules must be considered.

Another question has to be asked: Who is the identified patient? Who is the one who is hurting the most? In this situation there are two: Mrs. C. and her son. By identifying Mrs. C. as the one who is senile, the staff did not need to face further responsibility for considering alternate forms of care, and things could move along "normally." By identifying Mr. C. as a "troublemaker" and "complainer" whenever he came into the hospital, the presumably healthy portion of the system (the hospital staff) did not need to take his complaints seriously and consider other ways of dealing with the problem. The problem was "solved" by labeling the identified patients and then giving them routine care according to the label.

The final question has to do with identifying the problems, and asking why the family problem has not been solved and what needs to be done to bring about a solution. Here the counselor—and often the pastor is the only counselor available outside the family system—has to proceed carefully and intelligently. Options have to be considered. It may well be that the one problem Mrs. C.'s illness or behavior, may not be solvable. It may indeed be chronic brain syndrome from which there will be no relief until death, but the other option must also be considered. Is it a reversible condition brought on by a variety of factors—the shock of the two tragic losses, the unresolved grief work, the interacting medication?

Mr. C.'s problem also has several possible explanations. He felt powerless and probably misunderstood. The more he felt this way, the harder he tried to do something, and all he could do was complain. The more threatened by his complaints the staff felt, the harder they dug in their heels. So the vicious circle continued. Somehow this had to be broken. Out of considerations like this, goals for possible resolution are constructed.

In this particular incident, the counselor tried to help the various elements of the family system, the staff, and particularly Mr.

C., to look at the problem from a different vantage point, to open up some of the options. The counselor said:

> It seems to me that a major part of the problem with Mr. C. is that he just can't accept that his mother is being cared for as well as possible. . . . From his point of view, his mother was fine until she went into shock from finding her sister. . . . His problem, it seems to me, is that since he has never seen how his mother would be if she were not being cared for, he has no accurate basis for comparison.

With regard to the hospital staff, the counselor had to move very gingerly so as not to create rigid defensiveness by unwarranted criticism. So she went on to point out:

> I was looking for things an outsider might notice, but an insider wouldn't have time to think about. For example, in regard to medication, I noticed that the PRN [as needed] orders for medication were rather extensive; I understand the rationale for that.

The counselor then went on to discuss the various options for alternate medication, including the option of no medication at all as a "trial and error" method of seeing what constructive change might come about. It is important to note that changes of this sort must be taken with medical counsel and by a person who has a medical-skill orientation that most pastors do not have. If there had been a pastor in this particular system, he or she might well have been enlisted to support both the staff in considering changes and Mrs. C. as she was allowed to experience the full force of her grief without the dulling effect of the mood-altering drugs.

What finally did happen? The medication was altered and the staff was given further training in providing the kind of support Mrs. C. would need as she suffered her grief. The counselor conferred with Mr. C. and gained his informed consent for the temporary cessation of the sedation and provided him with support in the ensuing change. Mr. C. was enlisted in helping his mother retain reality orientation during her waking hours and was alerted that this would require his giving large blocks of time, day and night, for a few days.

As a result of these changes in medication and her son's attention, Mrs. C. regained her sense of orientation and was able to begin to work through her grief and resume some control of her life. On one of her first visits with Mrs. C., the counselor was "amazed to discover Mrs. C. sitting up in bed, reading the newspaper account of the Watergate hearings." Obviously this is almost a miraculous success story which did actually happen but which may not be typical. Yet it is an important case in demonstrating how important it is to take into account the total system of which the elderly person is a part and to consider aspects of care that may not always be obvious. Though no pastor was involved in this case, it is clear at how many points a caring pastor or a knowledgeable member of a congregation could have been helpful in bringing about the healing that eventually resulted.

Elders in the family system

Relationships become complex and sometimes intense for the whole family system in the three- or four-generational family. An increasing phenomenon is the three-generational family, with two of the generations being retired. The statistics tell the story. Between 1970 and 1976 the number of adults over 65 increased 14.8% in America. Those over 75 increased 16.1%, and those over 85 increased a massive 39.6%. Demographers tell us that the four- and five-generational family will become common as the number of persons reaching 85 years of age increases. This poses a variety of problems.

As costs of nursing-home care and Medicaid and Medicare increase, institutionalization of older people will become less possible or popular unless some radical changes are made. The alternative is for several generations of older people in the family to move in with each other, but this raises the issues of whose home shall be surrendered? Who is to be the head of the family? How will financing be arranged? And for those families that decide not to combine resources, how do they deal with the sense of responsibility if young retirees do not make a home for parents or even grandparents? It is quite likely that group living arrangements may be made laterally, with friends and colleagues, rather than with family members.

But all these solutions pose the need for new adjustments for members of the family system, whether or not they are living in the same building. Mr. and Mrs. K., who have been retired for five years, are currently in a dilemma as to how to properly care for Mr. K.'s mother, who married Mr. K.'s stepfather (Mr. B.) about five years ago. The elder couple are quite well-to-do, but Mr. B. is extremely "careful" about his money. Consequently the living arrangements and household management at Mr. and Mrs. B.'s is quite unsatisfactory, even dangerous. Little cooking is being done by Mother B., since she is partially blind. Mr. B. is completely blind and hard of hearing and, therefore, difficult to care for.

The younger Mr. and Mrs. K. visit regularly in their parents' home to do some routine housekeeping and laundry, but beyond that they feel not only helpless but frustrated as to what to do. They find themselves in the position of almost every couple in this sort of situation—as "parents" to their own parents.

Among the host of problems that this multigenerational family phenomenon generates, let us take a closer look at just this aspect of "parenting one's own parents," because it seems that the pastor most often gets requests for help in this.

Helen and Jim G., a middle-aged couple with two teenage children, thought it only right that they take in Jim's mother when Jim's father died. But they did not reckon with the family dynamics that were awakened by this move. Over the years Jim had conveniently forgotten the rather authoritarian manner of his mother; nor had Mother G. lost her need to control her environment as fully as possible. As his mother came to live with them, Jim began to remember the instances of her rigid control of even the family pets. Now he observed her wanting to control his children just as she had controlled hers years ago.

Shirley and Tim, the teenagers, were going to have none of it. As they chafed under Mother G.'s constant criticism, they began to stay away from home more and more. Tim began to experiment with drugs to get out from under the tension. Every mealtime became an encounter in which Mother would lecture Helen and Jim on "how they ought to run a household" and "what those two teenagers need is. . . . " Home life became more and more of a nightmare. Finally, in desperation and guilt, Jim called on their pastor and asked for help in dealing with the family situation.

Jim and his wife Helen wanted to do all they could to provide for the well-being of Mother G., but their good intentions could not overcome some destructive family patterns that became reactivated in the three-generational household. Often this is the case. Good intentions and an honest desire to do what is best, or what the Fourth Commandment seems to call for, are in themselves not sufficient to insure the desired outcome. In such a situation as this, pastors must be especially careful that they do not automatically invoke various moralisms and assume that thereby help has been given. What is needed, first of all, is to hear Jim out, to let him express his sense of wanting to help but finding it so difficult and frustrating to counter his mother's need to control. Jim will doubtless need to express also some feelings from his own childhood, reactions to his mother's controlling spirit. These now in part fuel his feelings of guilt and frustration. Often when members of a multigenerational family again live together in the household, the original family system is reactivated, together with all the positive and negative feelings of the past. The same "rules" of the family system are automatically invoked, even though they may no longer be relevant to the present situation. Often it is the pastor's task to help people become aware of this process, to clarify these old feelings, and to assess whether the old rules are useful or destructive.

All of this is best done within relationships of trust and respect between the pastor and the various members of the family. And it is usually useful, where practical, to engage in this exploration with all of the family members together. Such a "family council" may be the best way to deal with the old issues and the new realities that confront the family as they seek more helpful and comfortable ways of living together. Pastors are often in a unique position to bring this about because they have ready access to the home and to every member of the family by virtue of their position in the community of faith. The pastor's request to speak with all of the family members together will be far less threatening than if some external expert were to make this request.

This approach of "conjoint family" conferences was pioneered by John E. Bell already in 1951, and it has proven to be a useful approach even now, particularly with families of troubled adolescents. But only more recently (1965) has the family systems approach begun to be applied to multigenerational families. The first paper in the gerontological literature proposing the family interaction system in problems associated with aging appeared in 1966. Area mental-health associations are taking up this approach and are presenting workshops for the training of staff and interested pastors.

Several decades of experience of family therapists, as well as careful research, have identified a set of characteristic interactions within troubled families. Probably the most common of these is the process of *scapegoating*. Another type of interaction is *role inversion* or *role reversal*. This tends to occur somewhat naturally with middle-generation children who find themselves gradually becoming the parent of their parents, often out of necessity. In these instances the children take over the duties of parenting. Such role inversion also tends to regenerate some of the original conflicted relationships developed in the family of origin. Often I have found that when middle-aged children must parent their own parents, one of the things they attempt to do is to outshine their original parents. They are determined to do a better job of parenting than their own parents did. This generates natural feelings of guilt and resentment on both sides of the relationship. The reverse can also happen: the middle-aged parents now use the parenting role as an opportunity for revenge, to make up for real or perceived deprivations of childhood. The negative and destructive attitudes this generates can be easily imagined.

Still another problematic family interaction, quite closely related to role inversion, is the formation of *symbiotic relationships* in which the boundaries between parent and child (and inverted, child and parent) become blurred. Parents become so wrapped up in the lives of their children that they vicariously live through them. Such a pattern can persist throughout life, and it is not uncommon to find an elderly parent who cannot let go of his or her adult children, often making very unrealistic demands of the adult children. Such parents cannot allow their children to become adults and cannot give up the role of parenting. Such rigidity can, of course, cause havoc when elderly parents must be parented. Conversely, children, even up to middle-age, cannot let go of their parents, or let go of being dependent children, unable to separate their lives and being from those of their parents. When this occurs, middle-aged children may undergo severe disturbances when their elderly parents begin to decline and eventually die.

The opposite, in a sense, of such symbiosis is the occurrence of *extruded members* of the family—rejected members. This is an extreme form of scapegoating. Such extrusions often become manifest during ministry to dying elders. In concern to "get their house in order," the dying elder may be concerned about reconciliation with rejected members of the extended family. Elders themselves sometimes perceive institutionalization as a form of extrusion, and indeed this may sometimes be the case, though usually not with the frequency claimed. Society certainly practices this with extrusion of troublesome (sick, unproductive, "senile") elders who are simply "warehoused" in minimal care institutions to get them out of the way. Senior citizens housing complexes have something of this flavor as well.

In families having members of all ages, *dyadic alliances* may be established, which can be very healthy or very destructive. In essence this involves the teaming up of two members with each other; often relationships between a grandparent and a particular grandchild can be special in this sense, and usually very constructive. But a destructive alliance can occur in which it becomes "us against the family," taking forms of special favoritism ("you have a special place in my will") or the setting up of revenge systems ("we'll show them"). In such alliances the elder member may become the object of special attention and care by the partner in such a way as to demean other members of the family.

It is helpful for the pastor to be aware of these expressions of the family system and the patterns of interaction that get established, but these patterns of interaction should not be used as boxes in which people are placed (thus extruding them), assuming that analysis is the essence of helping. Analysis is never that; it is only a preliminary tool used to understand the problem better and to help indicate goals, decisions, and actions that are necessary to bring health and wholeness to the entire family system.

12

The Local Congregation Ministers to Elders

Ministry to older persons is not the private province of the ordained leader of the congregation. The ministrations of the pastor are best understood as the expression of the life and concern of the total community of faith—the congregation. The pastor is the incarnation, as it were, of the responsibility of the congregation to proclaim the gospel. The pastor is the individualized instrument used by the local congregation to proclaim the reconciling Word and to provide leadership and guidance in the nurture of the life of faith. Thus, ministry to elders is the province of the congregation as a whole. In this chapter we want to explore more fully this total ministry of the congregation.

One of the student-interns of a Lutheran seminary recounts this encounter with a person he described as "a formidable geriatric inquisitor," the 85-year-old mother of a parishioner the student was to visit:

> "So you're going to be a minister, eh? Tell me, how is your training?" After expressing her rather negative opinion of that training, she went on to say, "The clergy are a necessary nuisance in our society. We don't really want you around, but we tolerate you. You are there because Christians are lazy, and Christians are lazy because you are there. If you weren't around, there would be a lot more people who would have to take their faith more seriously."

In her cantankerous way this elderly grandmother raised the issue that is our concern: the relationship between the ministry of the designated pastor and the ministry of the whole congregation to older persons. She reflected an understanding of ministry that regards the ordained pastor as the one who is hired to do the congregation's work. Often, because of self-aggrandizing needs of our own, we clergy do regard ourselves as the only person capable of fulfilling the ministries that are needed by the congregation in its inspiration, nurture, and caring of its own members and its responsibilities to the larger community.

Thomas Oden notes, "All believers are called to witness to the gospel, visit the sick, serve the needy, and assist in the building up of the community. This general ministry is committed to every Christian" (he cites Matt. 5:16 and 28:18-20).[1] What is committed to each Christian individually is committed to the collective whole—the congregation. The pastor inspires, guides, facilitates, and implements this individual and collective ministry. Unfortunately the professionalism of ministry and the skewed perceptions of laity have served to obscure this understanding.

Ministry to elders in the local congregation

What is the ministry of the local congregation to older persons? Through personal experience, reflection, consultation with parish pastors and some knowledge of the needs of older persons, I have come to see this ministry as including four basic components:

1. The traditional ministry of Word and sacrament,
2. The ministry of information and referral,
3. The ministry of the ombudsman,
4. The ministry of advocacy,

All these components express the central concern and reason for the existence of the church created by the gospel: to proclaim God's dual passion for the world, that we may know his grace and that human beings may live together in justice. A fine expression of this mandate is the words of Isaiah:

> Behold my servant, whom I uphold,
> my chosen, in whom my soul delights;
> I have put my Spirit upon him,
> he will bring forth justice to the nations. . . .

I am the Lord, I have called you in righteousness,
  I have taken you by the hand and kept you;
I have given you as a covenant to the people,
a light to the nations,
  to open the eyes that are blind,
  to bring out the prisoners from the dungeon,
  from the prison those who sit in darkness.
I am the Lord, that is my name;
my glory I give to no other (Isa. 42:1, 6-8).

This is the *leitmotif* that Jesus himself accepted for his ministry, and it is the ministry he has entrusted to his church.

In this chapter we will discuss the first component of congregational ministry to elders, the traditional ministry of Word and sacrament. The other three components are discussed in Chapter 13.

The traditional ministry of Word and sacrament

The ministry of Word and sacrament is the primary ministry for all, but especially for older persons. They, more than any other age group, need to hear the objective Word of God coming to them from outside their reminiscings and ruminations, the erosions of hope, and the emerging fears that are so much a part of growing older. Especially as they become more and more marginal in the fabric of human relations and less obviously productive to the fellowship, they begin to doubt whether they are worth the blessings of salvation promised, or even whether the promises are intended for them.

For reasons unique to the experience of growing old, the proclamation of the reconciling Word is fundamental to any program of ministry to older people, especially the frail elderly. It is this living Word that distinguishes the church from other effective and competent social programs for older people.

One reason older people need the Word is their fear of abandonment. The issue of abandonment takes many forms. In the life of Mattie, it took the form of the question, "Is my life enough?" Mattie was born in 1907 into a black family. She managed to get to school and to earn a teaching degree, an unusual accomplishment in her time. She taught her own and other black children and was instrumental in sending many black children on to higher education. In addition, she raised a family, and after her family was grown, she raised a niece because her sister was ill. She saw to it that all her children were raised in the church. Seventy-five years later, she confessed to her visiting friend that she was still wondering whether her life was enough to merit God's loving grace. Whether the theology she heard proclaimed was a "bootstrap theology" or a theology of grace, we can only conjecture; apparently the gospel was not proclaimed with the clarity that it deserves. Yet even if it had been, the surrounding culture did much to erode the gospel. The question, Is my life enough? plagues even the most knowledgeable elder brought up in the purest proclamation of the gospel. Therefore it continues to be of utmost importance that the proclamation of the gospel in preaching and in church educational programs be unalloyed by any kind of bootstrap theology.

Surely one of the reasons why the original ministry of Jesus was addressed to the "down and out" and why the synoptic Gospels point out that it was the outcast and the poor to whom he proclaimed the kingdom was to make clear that this gospel is a gift from God, a blessing that can in no way be earned or purchased. These desperately poor—as only Third World persons can be poor—could in no way repay, yet they became citizens of the kingdom. Even when poor, elderly widows can no longer bring even a widow's mite, the gospel of God's grace is for them. This message must come again and again to our elders, particularly when they can no longer in any human sense be productive to the life and work of the congregation.

The means of proclaiming this gospel must extend beyond the general announcement of preaching. Elders need some tangible evidence that the generalized pronouncement of preaching does indeed include them. The regular preaching of the Word and the corporate worship of the congregation require supplementing by the ministry of the whole congregation through the personal witness of compassion, love, and concern. This takes shape in all sorts of common human kindnesses and forms of attention, both within the worship setting as well as in the daily lives of the people of the congregation.

It took place, for example, in the recent celebration of Mrs. B.'s 96th birthday in a small, rural congregation. During the morning worship, members of the children's choir gathered around the pew where Mrs. B. was sitting—far up front, for she was hard of hearing—and sang to her their anthem for the day. For all the congregation it was a moving participation in the celebration of the birthday of this elder saint, but it proclaimed a deeper message too: that the Word of grace was personally intended for her.

Personal attentions such as this, supplemented by drop-in visits of family and friends and careful attention to see that elders have shelter, heat, and food are all manifestations of this personalized concern. But in the life of the Christian congregation, where our concern is that the gospel be understood as personal grace and promise for the poorest and the oldest as well as the most active and the young, these personal attentions must go further than compassionate human concern. It must be made clear, both to those who extend these ministries as well as to the person receiving them, that these are forms of the gospel. Somehow it must be articulated that these ministrations represent and, in a sense, sacramentally convey the assurance that God's redeeming grace is still, and always will be, extended to the most frail, most helpless elder.

The traditional manner in which the generalized pronouncement of the liberating Word is particularized for individual elders has been the "pastoral call" or "shut-in visitation" for those who are homebound. Though it is traditional, it is often neglected or regarded as having lower priority than other pastoral functions. I have been forced to this conclusion based on the number of times I have been asked as a seminary professor, "Don't you teach the importance of pastoral visiting any more?" Indeed we do, but somewhere the message seems forgotten. This ministry to the homebound need not be, however, the private province of the pastor. It is a ministry in which any lay member of the congregation, properly prepared, can participate. An earlier book of mine, *The Compassionate Visitor* (Augsburg, 1984), is a resource to train lay visitors to visit ill and homebound persons. I have a suspicion that more regular calling on the homebound elderly does not take place because the pastoral visitors are not sure of the function of such visits. If a clear sense of purpose is lacking, then it is easy for the visitor to get bogged down in reminiscences and small talk. It is hoped that the suggestions offered here can help alleviate this difficulty and help revitalize and increase the pastoral contact of a congregation with its homebound members.

The main purpose of pastoral visitation, particularly to older members of the congregation, is to personalize the promise of the saving grace of our Lord Jesus Christ. The means by which this may be done are varied, but the message is the same: namely, that they are not cast off in the time of old age, or forsaken when their strength is spent (Ps. 71:9). This does not necessarily require a great deal of "God talk." But what must be done, somehow, is to make clear that the personal attention, the various forms of ministry, are all, directly or indirectly, expressions of God's care and grace, whether they are a daily check to see if the elder living alone is still alive and healthy, a warm meal, a friendly visit, a gift of food, an article of clothing, the delivery of medicine, some information on how to manage a report form, or help with a legal problem.

Direct evidence of God's care is provided by the very presence of the ministering persons, whoever they may be, ordained or not. When such lay visitors are expressly delegated for such visitation this evidence is clearer. What is needed, in addition, is evidence not only that God has not forgotten them, but that he regards them continually *with grace,* just as when they were young and actively contributing members of the congregation. This transcendent dimension of God's continued grace must be communicated as clearly as possible, and we shall discuss some ways of communicating this message shortly. But first, let us examine why this message is so important to the elder.

Here we touch upon the reason why many shut-in elders long for a visit from the pastor. Many pastors have been frustrated by this request, particularly when they have taken pains to organize a regular program of lay visitation for all the homebound members of the congregation. The pastor knows that the elders are getting their share of attention and are adequately cared for. Why do they want more? What is the more they wish? Why do they demand a pastoral visit? Simply because the symbolic or sacramental person of the pastor, as the "official" representative of the church and as the official ambassador of Christ (2 Cor.

5:20), carries this transcendent dimension, the evidence of God's continued grace.

It is not that the same reinforcement of the covenant of grace conveyed by any member of the body of Christ is less valid. The issue here is not one of theology, but of human perception. As Luther has said, we are all called to be, and capable of being, "little Christs" for each other. But this message or gift comes through with greater clarity with some "little Christs" than with others. The issue here is not that the word of an ordained person carries more validity or authenticity than the same word of a nonordained Christian. It is a matter not of validity or truth, but of perception. If a physician says to one troubled with arthritis, "Take some aspirin," it has more credibility than if a member of the family expresses the same medical advice. In both cases the message is true. In the one, the truth is more trustfully perceived. In this simple analogy it seems to me we understand something of the meaning of ordination, or special delegation, that we easily overlook.

Forms of the visible Word

For elders it is important that such words of care and blessing become as concrete as possible. Because so many of the frail elderly, particularly, live alone or have limited human contact, they begin to live very inward lives; they withdraw into their own memories and perceptions; they talk to themselves—figuratively at least, and often literally. Increasingly, the measure and range of reality is their own internal mental life. This is one reason why such elders sometimes have difficulty in distinguishing between reality (what's out there) and fantasy (what's in their own heads). Geriatric psychiatry is well aware of this and for this reason advises frequent "reality orientation" exercises and experiences for the frail elderly. Elders begin to wonder whether the promise made by children that they will come to visit at Thanksgiving or Christmas is a figment of their imagination, created by their own intense desire to see their children, or whether the children really did say it. Letters, therefore, are often a more valuable and important means of communication than telephone calls, because a letter can be reread.

The same thing can happen with the promises of grace; does God really *say* that he will not leave us nor forsake us, even when we are old, or is this just my own wishful thinking? This is why, for Luther, the church was a "mouth house" where the promise of God was *spoken* so it could be *heard, written* down in Scripture, so it could be *read,* and sacramentally given so it could be *tasted* and *felt.* This is why "The Word became flesh and dwelt among us" (John 1:14), so that it would never be corroded by our own wishful thinking or our fear that we are imagining things. A "visible word" in the person of a member of the Christian congregation takes on a sacramental quality, conveying in tangible form the continued, providential care of God. A "visible word" in the person of a commissioned ambassador of Christ who speaks a word of grace (which can be heard) and who lays a hand on a shoulder or offers a handclasp (which can be felt) conveys the grace of Christ in a sacramental way. This carries profound implications for the two major elements of traditional ministry, the individual pastoral call and the sacramental ministry of the congregation. Both of these have the potential of conveying the message of God's continued providential care and his redemptive concern.

Pastoral visits with homebound elders

The pastoral visit to the homebound elder can convey this message of providential care and redemptive love if it is intentionally planned for, whether conducted by pastor or designated parish visitor. If the visitor wishes to convey the personalized message of God's care and grace, this can often be done effectively by the "hand of blessing." By this is meant human touch accompanied by a word of blessing: "the grace of our Lord Jesus Christ, the love of God the Father, and the communion of the Holy Spirit be with you," the Aaronic blessing, or the passing of the peace, as provided for in many liturgies. The form of touch can be varied—a hand on the shoulder, a firm handclasp, or, if the person is lying down, a hand on the forehead while the blessing is spoken.

All these rituals will transmit the essential message which is the particular province of the church. This can be done routinely for elders who are part of the family of faith, members of the Christian congregation or other confessing Christians. Whether this blessing should be given to those who are not of the household of faith is a matter of judgment. This is not to say that God wishes to withhold such blessing from them, but questions rather whether such blessing will for them be meaningful or understandable, or even desired. When there has been some prior context that helps to make the blessing of grace meaningful, then, of course, it is appropriate.

Another way in which the gracious promise of God is made personal is through the use of Scripture and prayer as a part of the pastoral visit. One of the important functions of the pastoral visit with homebound elders is to give them a sense of connectedness to the worship life of the family of faith. The weekly pericopes are of great value in this regard; reading in the presence of the elder the lessons for the Sunday preceding the visit gives the elder a sense of sharing with the congregation in the promises of God. If the setting and context allow, the visitor may deal with the lesson as it was proclaimed from the pulpit. Or, one can discuss the lesson in the fashion of a Bible study, encouraging dialog and response on the part of the elder. When I visited elders I was often surprised to find how the lesson for the particular week spoke to the situation of the elder. This can be pointed out and mutually explored by the visitor and the elder. To be avoided is the routine or stiff and formal reading of general pericopes that have been chosen with little thought for the situation or spiritual state of the person being visited. In a certain sense, the whole of Scripture is for the pastor like the pharmacopoeia of the physician. To be able to use Scripture in this manner requires a good knowledge of it on the part of the pastoral visitor.

One should not hesitate to deal with profound theological issues in the use of Scripture with elders; they are hungry for deepening their knowledge and theological perception. Thus a straightforward educational use of the Bible is often appropriate. The visitor can also suggest books to be read, including sophisticated theological books for those who have the capability to digest them. I have the impression that pastors often underestimate the capability and spiritual appetites of their parishioners.

In a nursing-home setting the several members of the faith might be gathered together for a brief Bible study and discussion of matters of faith.

Another resource that helps the homebound member to feel a continuing part of the corporate family of worship is the use of other elements of the Sunday liturgy, particularly the Prayer of the Day, which is intended to collect the themes and concerns of the congregation and bring them before the throne of grace. Hymns used in the worship are also useful in this regard; they need not always be sung. Many pastoral visitors are not good soloists, and elders are often unable to sing any longer. The hymns may be read together.

A common practice is the use of audiotapes of the worship service. I recommend, however, some editing of these tapes; often the whole service is too long, particularly for a frail elderly person, so a good practice is to record only one or two stanzas of a hymn. Other editing will suggest itself to the sensitive visitor. Let me add that the use of tapes provides a good vehicle for the involvement of lay visitors; it gives them something concrete to form the backbone of a visit. I hope, however, lay visitors to the elders in the congregation will not just sit passively by and listen to the tape, but will feel free to engage in active conversation with the elder.

Regular mailing of the church bulletin and newsletters to homebound elders is another way to help the isolated elder feel a part of things that are going on. With normal caution against idle gossip, the pastor or lay visitor can also share other news about the congregational life—who is ill, who needs prayers, who might profit by a word of encouragement.

Homebound elders are eager to remain involved in the life of the congregation. They want to be a part of the ministry, giving and serving, as well as being the passive recipients of ministry. Older homebound persons can also engage in regular interces-sory prayer for members of the congregation, the pastor, and lay leaders; this amounts to a vocation for one who can in no other way contribute to the life of the parish. A prayer list pro-vided by the pastor can be the basis for a welcome and useful ministry by an elder. Older people can further personalize their involvement in concern for fellow members of the family of faith through use of the telephone, calling those who need a word of encouragement or appreciation and praise.

Sacramental ministry to homebound elders

For an aged Christian, receiving the bread and the wine of Holy Communion is the clearest way of gaining personalized assurance of the living Word of grace. In the eating and drinking of these "visible words" the renewed assurance is given that God has not abandoned the lonely and frail elder, now no longer capable of any response to the gift except a trusting open hand and opened mouth. Regular and reverent reception of this most blessed gift is therefore of prime importance to all the elder saints of the congregation. It is one of the pastoral ministrations that should have the highest priority for the ministry of the congregation and the pastoral staff.

Ideally, elders in the congregation will receive this sacrament along with all other members of the congregation at the regular worship services. But many elders are homebound and unable to assemble with the entire congregation around the Lord's table. These homebound elders are not to be forgotten when it comes to the celebration of the eucharistic meal. Provisions are made in the rituals of many congregations for the distribution of this sacramental gift by pastoral or lay members of the congregation.

Whether an ordained pastor, a lay member of the pastoral staff, or perhaps a deacon or other member of the church council distributes the elements is a matter of pastoral judgment. Many older members of our congregations have traditionally regarded sacramental ministry as one of the special domains of ordained clergy. That this may exhibit a less than adequate theological understanding of ordination is not the issue here; what is important is what the ministration itself conveys to the elder. To move too quickly to lay distribution of the sacrament can generate some confusion and misunderstanding in the mind of the elder as to whether their reception of the sacrament is truly valid. For this reason, careful interpretation and explanation of the procedure is always wise. It will be helpful to explain, for example, that the sacraments are not the private province of the ordained minister, but the gifts of the risen Lord to the church, of which the ordained pastor or the lay ministrant is the server. The validity of the sacraments does not rest in the one who serves them, but in the gift and promise of the risen Lord who instituted them.

In the past in large parishes, where the pastor could not regularly visit all homebound elders, the lonely elder had some assurance of a visit by the pastor when the sacrament was administered. These visits were looked forward to as an important sign that the "chief shepherd" of the congregation had not forgotten them and, indirectly of course, also a sign that the Lord, whose special servant the pastor is, had not forgotten them. Therefore, to assign the ministry of sacraments to designated lay visitors exclusively may convey the very opposite message that the sacraments themselves are intended to convey. Though we pastors may feel this special "pastoral aura" to be a cumbersome bit of baggage, to ignore this attitude and longing on the part of elders could be destructive to the spiritual welfare of those we serve. How one deals with this in the pastoral-care program of the individual congregation is therefore a matter that should be given careful pastoral consideration.

One of the messages the Lord's Supper conveys is that the recipient is enfolded once again and into the whole family of faith; the isolated homebound person becomes a part of the whole congregation. This message can be conveyed in a variety of ways, not the least of which is careful attention to the home worship setting. Every effort that is taken to make the communion service like that which the congregation assembled celebrates is helpful. This can include attention to the aesthetics of the table from which the elements are to be served, the vessels in which they are served, and the like. This is especially significant in the often drab setting of a nursing home or hospital room. Clean linens and aesthetically pleasing vessels do much to help make it the festive and significant service that it is. Usually with home-bound elders, time is not of the essence, so there is opportunity to take these factors into account. It is helpful for elders to have a manageable copy of the liturgy from which they can participate. Often a heavy hymnbook is unmanageable or hard to read. One pastor I know of prepares the communion liturgy in large type on bulletin folders that can be easily held by frail hands. Candles and a cross on a table spread with clean linen become an important witness. The use of taped hymns sung by the assembled congregation can also be edifying, though care should be used as to the length of the home service. Here, as in so much of pastoral work, the artfulness of a consecrated imagination is most useful.

One further way in which the isolated homebound elder can experience the fellowship of the saints is by having other members of the congregation or family join in the celebration of the Eucharist. Some denominations, particularly in the Reformed tradition, require that at least two members of the congregation be present at any "private communion." The term "private communion" is unfortunate, because it implies that this occasional service is somehow a private matter. This is fortunately being overcome by the contemporary emphasis that the homebound service is but an extension of the assembled congregation's celebration of the Lord's Supper.

Many congregations go to great lengths to make it possible for all homebound elders to be a part of the visible gathering of saints at communion services celebrated on the festivals of Christmas or Easter or Pentecost, by bringing them to the sanctuary in vans, ambulances, or wheelchairs. One church has special services for these people followed by a luncheon on two often-forgotten days that are important to elders—Reformation Day and Maundy Thursday.

Educational program of the congregation

The importance of continued learning and education for older members of our society and our congregations would be hard to overemphasize. Most major universities in the country now have continuing-education programs for persons over 65. It is no longer news when a grandmother or a grandfather earns a long-desired college degree. The same emphasis is equally valid in the life of faith. Older members of the congregation are eager to study the Bible and theology at a level that respects their intelligence. Such study and discussion in groups is being recognized as increasingly valuable by gerontologists. Whereas two decades ago group work with older persons was regarded as either difficult or unproductive, now group work with older persons—

including not only education but mutual support, self-awareness, and self-development—is regarded as very valuable. Group work of this sort can be a part of a fully developed parish program or the program of a church-related nursing home. Most community mental-health agencies and many Christian congregations are now sponsoring support groups among elders; for example, widow's and widower's support groups seem to be one of the best resources to help elders through one of the most difficult losses in life.

In 1963 the American Medical Association issued a report on medical aspects of aging which stated:

> A sense of purpose and the opportunity to contribute to others; these are as vital to total health as are adequate nutrition and rest. Whether this opportunity is thwarted by family members who deny the older members a voice in the family council, who are overprotective and relegate him to the role of "puttering," whether thwarted by the community which refuses to utilize the capabilities and contributions seniors can make to all aspects of community life; or whether thwarted by employers who refuse to hire after a certain age or retire persons at arbitrary chronological age . . . the results are equally detrimental to physical and mental health.

One of the social factors that thwarts the contribution or ministry of the older person is the tendency toward age segregation. We segregate ourselves by age in housing patterns by putting elders in rest homes and young married couples in suburbs, in entertainment patterns by catering to adolescent tastes in public media, by work patterns with retirement policies, and in congregations by tightly graded church schools. In the era of the extended family—if it ever truly existed as we idealize it—there was opportunity for cross-generational interaction, for children to make contributions of wonder and wisdom to elders and for elders to contribute perseverance and poise to children. We idealize this era because somehow we sense that is the way "things ought to be." The congregation has often been described—and idealized—as an extended family; whether or not that be the case, it is a setting in which cross-generational experiences can be fostered.

Cross-generational experiences can occur in the worship life and in the educational program of the congregation. Bible classes, courses in modern social problems, family-life education, and Christian theology are some possibilities. In the so-called primitive culture of the Zulus, for example, family-life educating of the young was not done by parents, but was done by aunts and uncles or grandmothers and grandfathers. There is much wisdom in jumping one generation to find educators in this sensitive area. In spite of all kinds of available information and a congenial cultural climate, many parents still find it difficult to discuss sexual matters with their children or to halt the epidemic rate of teenage pregnancies. Some are concluding that parents are not the persons to be doing the family life and sex education, that it should be done by the elders or other members of the extended family. Some congregations have experimented with programs of family life and sex education in which teenagers and grandparents learned in the same class. Certainly the same benefits could occur in a well-designed program of Bible study or study of Christian faith. Some congregations are making use of a mentor program in confirmation instruction or preparation for adult church membership. In these programs an older person of the "grandparent generation" volunteers to become a mentor for an adolescent who is receiving confirmation instruction. The youth has the opportunity to select a mentor from those who have volunteered for the program. The role of the mentor varies from being one of the primary teachers to functioning as an advisor or someone with whom the youth can discuss questions and problems.

Another significant cross-generational program is the gathering of oral histories. Young people interview older members of the congregation to get the history of the community or of the congregation. These conversations are taped and become a part of the congregational or community archives.

A mission congregation in Casper, Wyoming, began its life by holding services in the chapel of a rest home in the area. As the congregation grew, the time came to consider building a sanctuary. Instead, the congregation decided to continue worshiping in the chapel of the rest home and build only an educational unit nearby. The congregational contact with the elders in the home was felt to be too valuable to lose. In another rest home in Nor-walk, California, there is a day nursery adjacent to the home, staffed almost entirely by residents of the home. In Australia it is typical for congregations to have both a small group home for elder living and a day nursery on the campus of the church. The nursery is staffed largely by elders, and children have ready access to visiting their "grandmothers" and "grandfathers" at the home. Family camping is another rich opportunity for cross-generational experiences in which children, their parents, and members of the "grandparent" generation attend the camp at the same time. Patterns and opportunities for cross-generational experiences within the traditional parish program are rich and varied, limited only by the boundaries of the imagination of elders and their pastoral leaders.

Ministry to the dying elder

The lifelong pilgrimage of aging ends in death. We do not always like to face that and in our culture go to great lengths to avoid it, but it is true nevertheless. An important ministry for older persons can be pastoral work that transforms death from dreaded enemy to at least possible friend, if not welcome guest. The long-range ministry of the pastor to older persons must include preparing them for "a good death," as much as possible.

There is a more specific preparation for death that we want to consider now: ministry to the older person who in a literal sense is facing death because of terminal illness or severe trauma. I shall do this only briefly here, for more detail on ministry to the dying I have provided elsewhere.[2] The first component of such a ministry is the pastor's own willingness, composure, and ability to talk with elders about their dying. This is never easy for the minister. Though it is not easy for the elders either, they often are eager to talk to somebody about their dying. Such conversations may be encouraged, perhaps even initiated, by the pastor. Knowing when and whether the elder is ready for such a conversation is a matter of pastoral art born of experience, made easier often by the background of longer relationships and a backlog of earlier conversations. The best guide is the willingness and the capacity of the elder to engage in such conversations, evidenced often by little hints and veiled questions.

It will be helpful if the pastor can also prepare other members of the family to share in these conversations about impending death. Most harmful is the lonely isolation that can occur when family members are afraid to broach the subject or even go so far as to try to keep secret from the elder the reality of coming death. As much as possible the pastor should endeavor to break through this conspiracy of silence by working with the family so that they can endure the difficult ministry of sharing death with an elder member of the family.

In these conversations with the dying elder, care should be taken to be gently honest as much as is possible; that means answering whatever questions the elder may raise about death. Often the pastor must say, "I don't know." For Christians, the best resource in these conversations is the resurrection hope we have through our Savior. Again and again we will be brought back to the promises of eternal life, not as a way of avoiding death but of journeying through it into the mysteries of fulfillment of life promised to us in the gospel. One of the most helpful aspects of the resurrection faith that elders especially appreciate is the knowledge that Christ himself has gone through the pilgrimage of dying, and that he now accompanies us, even through death.

Many studies done in recent years identify dying as a process with several components. Dr. Elizabeth Kübler-Ross has identified the components of denial, anger, bargaining, depression, and acceptance.[3] (We would add the component of hope.) Sometimes these have been identified as successive stages that a person moves through in fairly orderly fashion. This is misleading. These components are analytical concepts that help us to understand what people are going through, not sequential steps that follow one after another. Knowing them helps us from being shocked when we observe them and enables us to walk alongside the dying person. We will likely find that a person moves back and forth from one component to another. Usually the dying person can reach deeper levels of acceptance of the reality of death as they are helped through the shock, the wish for a miracle, and grieving at giving up their life. They can pass through the valley of the shadow of death to emerge into acceptance and even hope.

During this time of dying the elder may prefer quiet companionship without much talking, or even solitude. Often there is a desire for the slowing down of personal relationships. Fewer visitors will be desired—perhaps none at all except for close family members. The dying person may have little energy for starting new relationships or maintaining fragile ones. The dying person may need to rest quietly in the durable relationships that life has given.

Ministry now is primarily a matter of presence. Conversation may be impossible, but presence is essential. There is a place for the quiet reading of favorite passages of Scripture, hymns, or poetry. Listening to music, particularly the hymnody of the church, may be especially meaningful. Though the dying person may not be able to respond by talking, remember that the sense of hearing lingers on after other senses have deteriorated. If the person is bilingual, Scripture, hymns, or prayers in the "mother tongue" may become particularly meaningful.

During the hours of dying, pastoral visits should be short and, if possible, more frequent. Personal contact, touching, the hand of blessing become important symbols of presence, comfort, and hope. The use of a fairly formal benediction with laying on of hands is also a useful way to communicate the abiding presence of God, the conqueror of death.

13

A *Triad of Innovative Ministries*

The triad of ministries suggested in this chapter moves beyond the traditional congregational ministry to older persons. Because they are concerned with the whole life of the people of God and the larger community, congregations have become concerned with issues such as housing, physical and emotional health, safety against crime, and justice for all members of society. All of these issues have long been the concern of the Christian church. What is being suggested here, then, is not entirely new, but what may be different is the organization of these ministries by the congregation to elders, and the opportunities for ministry by elders.

The social concerns of the congregation, particularly as they affect older members, can be fulfilled by three closely related, yet distinct, functions: providing appropriate and accessible information and referral services to elders, offering assistance in the use of these services through an ombudsman, and, finally, an advocacy program that seeks to ensure justice for elders.

The ministry of information and referral

Recently a senior citizen telephoned the community information and referral center in a rather confused state. A worker went out to see her. The elderly woman asked for help with her property tax forms; she thought she was eligible for a tax rebate check. It turned out that what she was puzzled about was a bill for her electricity. Because of her confusion about what the bill was for, she had not paid it and her electricity was due to be shut off.

Anyone who has experienced the intricacies of getting started on Social Security or Medicaid or Medicare is well aware of how difficult it can be when one goes for information to any of the public bureaus. One may be shunted from one office to another, sometimes treated as though one is ignorant or already senile. Yet this is a point in life of elders when they especially need the sense of respect and dignity.

With each succeeding generation in our society, the range of social-welfare, legal-aid, community-housing, health, and educational agencies is increasing at an astounding rate. When those who are elders today were young, there were only a few agencies for emergency assistance to older people. If the elder was indigent, he or she was put on county welfare or sent to the county farm, both experiences that were very demeaning. If you needed legal assistance, you went to a lawyer; if you were sick, to the doctor, usually a general practitioner; if you were mentally ill, you were sent to the state hospital for the insane.

Today the situation is far more complex, and as a consequence most elders are not aware of the wide range of agencies and resources that are available to provide help. They react with a mixture of bewilderment or shame for having to depend on these agencies—or else the feeling that the world owes them something, which creates dependency and corrodes personal dignity.

In this situation the church has an opportunity for a significant ministry for its elder members. Rather than attempt to duplicate services already provided in the community, a congregation or a group of congregations could provide information and refer elders to services already available.

A parish could have a volunteer or part-time staff member whose sole responsibility would be to develop a directory of community, state, and federal agencies that provide services to older people. Such an information bank would include the services offered by each agency, the eligibility requirements, fees, and entry procedures. In charge of gathering this information and making it available could be some trusted person in the congregation who could be called on for advice as to where to go for needed help and how to proceed. How helpful and comforting it could be to elders to know of just one person to call whenever help was needed beyond that which personal resources or family can provide. Every parish pastor that I know would be delighted to have such a resource person available to assist in the dozens of emergencies that arise month after month that call for just this sort of knowledge. Every parishioner and every family in a congregation would rest easier knowing that there is such a trustworthy source of information available, from a trustworthy person whose integrity and willingness to help is motivated by the love of Christ. Such a service would be a tremendous witness to the larger community that the church is indeed a caring community. Since a service of this sort would be open to all who called upon it, there is also a significant evangelism opportunity here.

A lay ministry such as this might well be the vocation of a retired social worker or a social-studies teacher, someone with knowledge of the wide range of resources available in any community. This volunteer staff person should be someone who has good organizational ability, is a good communicator, and can advise without being condescending or manipulative.

The functions of this person could include gathering information, investigating, communicating, counseling, and linking. In addition to cataloging information and making it readily available to elders, this person might visit many of the agencies and services listed to get acquainted with staff, discover from personal experience what is being offered, and gain some sense of the quality of services available. Such firsthand knowledge enables one to be a trustworthy helper. Communicating the gathered information might require creating a pamphlet, building a library, or setting up a round-the-clock telephone service. An important aspect of communication would be to teach the congregation and the community about the resources available and how to make best use of them.

The liaison includes linking the elder with needed services; linking the congregation with the resources, especially those that are church-related; and, finally, linking the helping agencies with people who need help—sometimes called "case finding." Particularly in larger cities there are countless hidden elderly who live alone, often in deteriorating hotels, in need of meals, medical aid, or legal assistance that agencies are mandated and willing to give if they but know of the persons who need their help. Of particular importance is the linking of the congregation to the various community rest homes, especially those that are church-related.

The ministry of the ombudsman

The ministry of the parish ombudsman is closely related to that of information and referral. The particular functions of the ombudsman (or ombudswoman) are: to serve as a "cutter of red tape," to lead an older person through the bureaucratic maze often confronted in an effort to get help, to be an advisor to straighten out what are often very tangled human problems, and finally to serve as a broker of volunteer services.

In smaller congregations the functions of ombudsman and information and referral could be combined in the same person. It is often helpful not only to know *where* to go, but *to whom* to go within a given agency. Or, given a variety of places where one might go to find a part-time postretirement job, one can often cut through the red tape and go to a particular agency or individual, if you know the ropes. This would be the task of the ombudsman.

The ombudsman can often be helpful in straightening out problems, for example, in legal and financial matters. Assisting an elder in the management of financial affairs is a similar matter, though not as technical, as a bank trust officer. In matters that have legal implications the ombudsman could be helpful in making the proper referral to a lawyer, or assist in dealing with the probate courts, or even function as a court-appointed guardian. Another area of help is in making a will, helping the person think through and gather necessary information before going to a lawyer. Often the pastor is called upon to be instrumental as a guardian or in the making of wills. But in order to protect the nature of the pastoral relationship, both functions should be avoided. A person related to the life and ministry of the church in the capacity of friend, however, could be welcomed both by the court and the individual.

The ombudsman should also have close contact with a wide variety of agencies. Because of this contact this worker would also have knowledge of opportunities in the community for volunteer service which members of the congregation might provide. So he or she might function as a "broker" to link interested and capable volunteers to the particular agency where they might make the best contribution. A related ministry of the ombudsman might be recruiting and training congregation volunteers for the ministry of the church in the wider community.

Because many elders are fearful of contact with professional persons and particularly of governmental agencies, the ombudsman might be called upon to accompany them as they go to get help and might also see that the elder is accorded the respect and courtesy important to every human being.

The ombudsman ought, then, to be someone also knowledgeable of governmental, state, legal, financial, and church-related resources for the assistance of older persons. The ombudsman will need compassionate understanding and good interview skills to determine the needs of an elder. Ability to improvise with patience and imagination would also be important.

The ministry of advocacy

The Christian community has not always been fully aware of the fact that God's passion for justice is as strong as his passion for redemption and grace.

The letter to the Hebrews describes Christ as our "advocate before the Father," the one who pleads our cause before the throne of judgment, desiring justice and mercy. In our time advocacy is one of the primary ways in which we as individual Christians and as congregations can join in God's concern for justice. Every Christian congregation ought to become known in the community and neighborhood as a place where those who are concerned for justice gather to worship the Lord of justice. Every congregation ought to be a haven where anyone—and particularly the elderly, because they are so often victims of injustice—might go for recourse to get justice.

This advocacy role of the congregation requires leadership, which can come from the pastor, but requires lay leadership as well. This can be supplied by an "advocacy officer" who, like the information and referral person and the ombudsman, becomes skilled in the specialized ministry.

The primary functions of the advocate fall into three areas: the correction of injustice, the positive pursuit of justice, and prevention of injustice. The elderly are often the victims of crimes of assault resulting in bodily harm or loss of property as well as crimes of fraud and deception. The congregational advocate ought to be constantly alert to the threat of crime in the community. When such crimes against the elderly occur, the advocate could be called upon to assist the elder in obtaining the proper legal or police help. The advocate would press for the prosecution of offenders, perhaps even organizing elders to be court watchers when crimes against the elderly are tried. Several years ago, as 20 elderly persons looked on, a 19-year-old youth who had beaten and robbed an 82-year-old woman of $2 was denounced as a predator and received the maximum sentence for his crime. When an elderly member of the congregation has been the victim of a crime, the advocate would function as "friend in court" of both elder and family.

The advocate would be constantly on the alert for fraudulent operators—household repairmen, door-to-door salesmen with "bargains," overpriced insurance policies, quack medical remedies, exploitive doctors, hospitals, and funeral parlors, and the like. One of the most widespread areas of fraud one state insurance regulator has called "mediscare" insurance, about which the advocate ought to warn elders.

The advocacy volunteer of the congregation has a positive role as well: to encourage fair and equitable treatment of older persons in all arenas of life. A commonly ignored problem in our society is that the total environment is largely planned for younger people, who are assumed to have perfect vision, total health, and no handicaps. The advocate could encourage better lighting for streets, compensation for victims of violent crime, protective measures for apartment laundry rooms and subway trains or buses, appropriate medical costs, or adequate Social Security benefits. The advocate should establish clear priorities, based on the community situation, and advise both congregation and community which of the endless causes ought to be fought for. Such advice would be welcomed by pastors, who often are over-whelmed with issues and causes the congregation or they personally ought to support.

Finally, the advocate could organize the congregation or the community, particularly the elder members, in volunteering as advocates, whether that be crime watchers in the community, court watchers, or lobbyists or demonstrators before city hall or a local fraudulent business. Close ties with such elder advocacy groups as Grey Panthers could be helpful.

What we have been suggesting in this chapter goes beyond the traditional ministry to elders. It is a ministry of the church, nevertheless, to be concerned that elders get the help that is needed in areas of life beyond the spiritual. As a caring community, the congregation is concerned about the whole of life of each of its members. Rather than attempt to provide such services itself, the church does far better to make sure that the community provides them and that knowledge about their availability is communicated to membership. Accordingly, we have suggested three functions of congregational ministry to elders: information and referral services, ombudsman assistance, and advocacy for justice. In smaller congregations these three functions might well be carried forward by one person; in larger congregations or congregations in larger communities, the three functions are distinct and demanding enough to offer a significant Christian vocation to any member of the congregation, but particularly the "young old."

On the wider front, I would hope that each of our church-related social-welfare agencies, hospitals, nursing homes, or other agencies that serve older persons might have similar staff persons who would be linked with, and perhaps even train and supervise, local congregational volunteers. National church offices might provide local volunteers with information, guidance, and inspiration so that the work of the Lord could be more effectively accomplished.

Appendix

How do you feel about growing older?

The inventory in Chapter 1 measures factual information and, by implication, attitudes and feelings about aging. There is need also for some way of assessing our own attitudes and opinions about the aged and about our own aging. This is best done in an extended discussion or exploratory interview or through rigorous self-examination. Inventories, however, can help in this process. The following inventory developed by the Ontario (Canada) Department of Social and Family Services is one of the more helpful of these that I have been able to find.[1] It not only measures the presence of a given attitude but gives some indication of its intensity.

> The statements below are opinions. You can identify opinions about each statement by circling some number between 1 and 10. Circling a 1 means that you very much agree, circling a 10 means that you very much disagree with the statement. Circling a 5 means that you have no opinion one way or another.
>
> | | *Agree* | *Disagree* |
> |---|---|---|
> | 1. Some people stay young at heart no matter how long they live. | 1 2 3 4 5 | 6 7 8 9 10 |

2. No one who is retired and over 70 should be allowed to drive a car. 1 2 3 4 5 6 7 8 9 10

3. Retired people are happiest in the company of people who are their own age. 1 2 3 4 5 6 7 8 9 10

4. Anyone could keep young if he only tried. 1 2 3 4 5 6 7 8 9 10

5. I cannot help feeling depressed at the thought of getting old. 1 2 3 4 5 6 7 8 9 10

6. You can't expect old people to exert themselves. 1 2 3 4 5 6 7 8 9 10

7. When you retire you realize that the best years of life are yet to come. 1 2 3 4 5 6 7 8 9 10

8. You'll never get old if you don't let yourself go. 1 2 3 4 5 6 7 8 9 10

9. It is rather sad to be still alive after all your friends are gone. 1 2 3 4 5 6 7 8 9 10

10. The future is so uncertain that there is little point in thinking of planning ahead. 1 2 3 4 5 6 7 8 9 10

11. All community organizations should have some older persons on their boards. 1 2 3 4 5 6 7 8 9 10

12. It must be a shock to look in the mirror and find that you are showing signs of aging. 1 2 3 4 5 6 7 8 9 10

Scoring Instructions: There are three attitudes which are measured in this inventory. Place the number which you have circled measuring your agreement or disagreement with the item in the box beside the item number. Multiply the number you entered by the weight number and place this result in the Score Box.

Attitude 1
Denial of aging

Item #	Raw score	Weight	Score
4		1	
7		1	
8		1	

Total _____

Attitude 2
Anxiety about one's own aging

Item #	Raw score	Weight	Score
5		4	
9		3	
10		2	
12		4	

Total _____

Attitude 3
Favorable or unfavorable
response to older persons

Item #	Raw score	Weight	Score
1		2	
2		4	
3		2	
6		2	
11		1	

Total _____

Scoring

The range of scores varies with each of the three attitudes measured. In Attitude #1: Denial of Aging, the range of possible scores is from 3 to 27. The lower the score, the greater the degree of denial. If, for example, your score total for Attitude #1 was 15, you are in the mid-range of denial. If you score 10 or under, you are engaging in considerable denial of the aging process.

In Attitude #2: Anxiety About One's Own Aging, the range of scores is from 13, the highest possible degree of anxiety, to 117, very low anxiety. A total score of 65, for example, is again "mid-range." Any score under 45 would indicate considerable anxiety about one's own aging. Likewise a very high score would indicate such a low degree of anxiety that it is likely you are engaging in some denial of the aging process. It would be well, therefore, to compare scores on these first two attitudes because they are interrelated.

In Attitude #3: Favorable or Unfavorable Response to Older Persons, the range of scores is from 9, a most unfavorable response to elders, to a high of 81, most favorable response. A total score of 44 is mid-range. It is likely that a score of around 30 and below indicates strong aversion to older persons, and this should be correlated with either high anxiety about one's own aging or denial. An unusually high score would probably be paired with a high anxiety score, while a very low score should be "tested" by the denial scale. A very low score might also indicate denial.

We do not have precise comparative statistics for an American population; the original scale was developed in Canada. While a comparison with a Canadian population might be interesting, it has not been included here because we are not really intending a highly statistical treatment of the issue in this book.

It might be most useful to develop norms for one's own congregation or study. What is desirable in parish education on aging is not only the dissemination of appropriate and correct information, but a change of attitude in those instances where individuals are denying or are anxious about their own aging.

It can be helpful to examine each of the items in this opinion survey for what it reveals about one's feelings toward the aging process. Some of the attitudes are more destructive to one's own aging and one's response to other older persons than others. There is space here for only a most cursory examination, to point out what may be particularly destructive.

1. Some people do indeed stay more or less "young at heart" no matter how long they live, but to hold this up as the ideal for all older persons, as total agreement would require, serves the

fantasy that all old people should be similarly pleasant and attractive to us and does not allow for those who will grow old
differently. There is a flavor of the youth-adulating culture here
as well, which ought to be rejected.

2. This idea rests on the stereotype that older persons have
more accidents than youth. The facts indicate otherwise, as has
been pointed out in the factual inventory (see item #8). To
strongly hold to this view is once more to believe that all older
persons are the same.

3. This attitude is a clear reflector of agism, which, like racist
prejudices, holds that people should be with their own kind. This
then means that I don't have to deal with them, because I'm not
like them.

4. This item reveals a "blame the victim" mentality: it is the
older person's own fault if he fails to remain young. To hold
strongly to this opinion suggests that youth is the ideal and aging
is negative.

5. Everyone is unhappy with his age, whatever it may be, at
some time or other in life. What adolescent has not wished she
were five years older, or younger? At times in life there seems
to be just no right age. Occasional depression, therefore, about
growing older is a normal and healthy aspect of aging. Constant
depression, a high agreement with this item, indicates a rejection
of aging, perhaps some fear of it, and therefore the probability
that one cannot realistically deal with growing older.

6. This attitude reflects what Martin Marty has observed in
a historical review of attitudes about aging: that aging has become
a social problem. Older people can be seen as the dependent
burdens for family or society. As has been pointed out, even some
of the current studies on aging can be seen as emphasizing older
people as a problem, as people to be taken care of. While this
may be partly true, we should not care in such a way as to deter
or prevent people from assuming responsibility for themselves.

7. This item reveals the myth of the "golden years." For some,
retirement years are the best years. For others, the vocational
years were the best; for still others, the high school years. All
people are individuals, and life experiences confront each of us
differently.

8. This item, too, measures denial of the aging process; it rests on the myth of the absolute value of youthfulness. It assumes that aging is almost due to some personal neglect, whether that be cosmetic, dietary, or failure to jog a mile a day. It assumes that we are in absolute personal control of what happens to us, even our growing old.

9. It is indeed sad to be alive after all your friends are gone. This is one of the more severe losses, particularly for the frail elderly, but it is not total loss. To hold this view assumes that one cannot gain new friends as one grows older. The experience of retirees who have moved from their lifelong home into new communities demonstrates that one can gain new friends and acquaintances up until the very last hours of life.

10. This item measures anxiety about aging and, in a broader sense, about the future as a whole. Admittedly, there is much in our time to be anxious about, and as one contemplates the future with the constant threat of nuclear destruction (to name only one issue), one can well be anxious. But to agree strongly with this item may indicate not only lack of courage to face the future, but lack of any spiritual faith that can sustain a person's pilgrimage into the future, an attitude which has significant pastoral implications.

11. One can certainly see the wisdom of having older persons on the board of most community agencies, but to insist that *all* should or should not once more fails to make important distinctions about the older persons who might serve or the nature of the community organizations. This item also measures one's attitude about the capability of older persons serving the community.

12. This item measures one's own anxiety about aging. Like most of the other items in this scale, it reflects the adulation of youth that infects us all. It can be a shock to discover wrinkles, but it is a shock from which one can recover if one has a healthy perspective on becoming an elder.

Inventories such as these have several uses in parish life and ministry. They might first be used by the pastor and others who have professional responsibilities in ministry to older persons to expose misinformation, prejudices, and attitudes that might hamper effective ministry. The inventories can also be used in study and discussion groups as a way of exposing stereotypes and prejudices and enlivening discussion about some of the most critical aspects of aging. They are an excellent way to open the subject of aging with any group, as well as a way of measuring change of attitudes and perceptions following a study of aging.

Difficult as it may be, it is important for the pastor, and for every aging person, to face one's own aging. One's experience and attitudes can be either a serious barrier or a real asset in effective ministry with and for older people.

The dying person's bill of rights

I have the right to be treated as a living human being until I die.

I have the right to maintain a sense of hopefulness however changing its focus may be.

I have the right to be cared for by those who can maintain a sense of hopefulness, however changing this might be.

I have the right to express my feelings and emotions about my approaching death in my own way.

I have the right to participate in decisions concerning my care.

I have the right to expect continuing medical and nursing attention even though "cure" goals have been changed to "comfort" goals.

I have the right not to die alone.

I have the right to be free from pain.

I have the right to have my questions answered honestly.

I have the right not to be deceived.

I have the right to have help from and for my family in accepting my death.

I have the right to die in peace and dignity.

I have the right to retain my individuality and not be judged for my decisions which may be contrary to beliefs of others.

I have the right to discuss and enlarge my religious and/or spiritual experiences, whatever these may mean to others.

I have the right to expect that the sanctity of the human body will be respected after death.

I have the right to be cared for by caring, sensitive, knowledgeable people who will be able to gain some satisfaction in helping me face my death.[2]

Residents' rights for persons living in long-term care facilities

(A) The rights of residents of a home shall include, but are not limited to, the following:

(1) The right to a safe and clean living environment pursuant to Titles XVIII and XIX of the "Social Security Act," 49 Stat. 620 (1935), 42 U.S.C. 301, as amended, and applicable state laws and regulations prescribed by the public health council;

(2) The right to be treated at all times with courtesy and respect, and full recognition of dignity and individuality;

(3) Upon admission and thereafter the right to adequate and appropriate medical treatment and nursing care and to other services that comprise necessary and appropriate care consistent with the program for which the resident contracted, without regard to considerations such as race, color, religion, national origin, age, or source of payment for care;

(4) The right to have all reasonable requests and inquiries responded to promptly;

(5) The right to have clothes and bed sheets changed as the need arises, to ensure the resident's comfort and sanitation;

(6) The right to obtain from the home, upon request, the name and any specialty of any physician or other person responsible for the resident's care or for the coordination of care;

(7) The right, upon request, to be assigned, within the capacity of the home to make the assignment, to the staff physician of the resident's choice, and the right, in accordance with the rules and written policies and procedures of the home, to select as the attending physician a physician who is not on the staff of the home. If the cost of a physician's services is to be met under a

federally supported program, the physician shall meet the federal laws and regulations governing such services.

(8) The right, in accordance with the rules of the home, to communicate with the physician in planning the resident's treatment or care and to obtain from the attending physician complete and current information concerning medical condition, prognosis, and treatment plan, in terms the resident can reasonably be expected to understand; the right of access to all information in his medical record; and the right to give or withhold informed consent for treatment after the consequences of that choice have been carefully explained. When the attending physician finds that it is not medically advisable to give the information to the resident, the information shall be made available to the resident's attorney or to the sponsor on the resident's behalf, if the sponsor has a legal interest or is authorized by the resident to receive the information. The home is not liable for a violation of this division if the violation is found to be the result of an act or omission on the part of a physician selected by the resident who is not otherwise affiliated with the home.

(9) The right to withhold payment for physician visitation if the physician did not visit the resident;

(10) The right to confidential treatment of personal and medical records, and the right to approve or refuse the release of these records to any individual outside the home, except in case of transfer to another home, hospital, or health care system, as required by law or rule, or as required by a third-party payment contract;

(11) The right to privacy during medical examination or treatment and in the care of personal or bodily needs;

(12) The right to refuse, without jeopardizing access to appropriate medical care, to serve as a medical research subject;

(13) The right to be free from physical or chemical restraints or prolonged isolation except to the minimum extent necessary to protect the resident from injury to himself, others, or to property and except as authorized in writing by the attending physician for a specified and limited period of time and documented in the resident's medical record. Prior to authorizing the use of a physical or chemical restraint on any resident, the attending physician shall make a personal examination of the resident and

an individualized determination of the need to use the restraint on that resident.

Physical or chemical restraints or isolation may be used in an emergency situation without authorization of the attending physician only to protect the resident from injury to himself or others. Use of the physical or chemical restraints or isolation shall not be continued for more than twelve hours after the onset of the emergency without personal examination and authorization by the attending physician. The attending physician or a staff physician may authorize continued use of physical or chemical restraints for a period not to exceed thirty days, and at the end of this period and any subsequent period may extend the authorization for an additional period of not more than thirty days. The use of physical or chemical restraints shall not be continued without a personal examination of the resident and the written authorization of the attending physician stating the reasons for continuing the restraint.

If physical or chemical restraints are used under this division, the home shall ensure that the restrained resident receives a proper diet. In no event shall physical or chemical restraints or isolation be used for punishment, incentive, or convenience.

(14) The right to the pharmacist of the resident's choice and the right to receive pharmaceutical supplies and services at reasonable prices not exceeding applicable and normally accepted prices for comparably packaged pharmaceutical supplies and services within the community;

(15) The right to exercise all civil rights, unless the resident has been adjudicated incompetent pursuant to Chapter 211 of the Revised Code and has not been restored to legal capacity, as well as the right to the cooperation of the home's administrator in making arrangements for the exercise of the right to vote;

(16) The right to consume a reasonable amount of alcoholic beverages at his own expense, unless not medically advisable as documented in his medical record by the attending physician or unless contradictory to written admission policies;

(17) The right to use tobacco at his own expense under the home's safety rules and under applicable laws and rules of the state unless not medically advisable as documented in his medical

record by the attending physician or unless contradictory to written admission policies.

(18) The right to retire and rise in accordance with his reasonable requests, if he does not disturb others or the posted meal schedules and upon the home's request remains in a supervised area, unless not medically advisable as documented by the attending physician;

(19) The right to observe religious obligations and participate in religious activities; the right to maintain individual and cultural identity; and the right to meet with and participate in activities of social and community groups at the resident's or the group's initiative, unless not medically advisable as documented in his medical record by the attending physician.

(20) The right upon reasonable request to private and unrestricted communications with his family, social worker, and any other person, unless not medically advisable as documented in his medical record by the attending physician, except that communications with public officials or with his attorney or physician shall not be restricted. Private and unrestricted communications shall include, but are not limited to, the right to:

  (a) Receive, send, and mail sealed, unopened correspondence;
  (b) Reasonable access to a telephone for private communications;
  (c) Private visits at any reasonable hour.

(21) The right to assured privacy for visits by the spouse, or, if both are residents of the same home, the right to share a room within the capacity of the home, unless not medically advisable as documented in his medical record by the attending physician;

(22) The right upon reasonable request to have room doors closed and to have them not opened without knocking except in the case of an emergency or unless not medically advisable as documented in his medical record by the attending physician;

(23) The right to retain and use personal clothing and a reasonable amount of possessions, in a reasonably secure manner, unless to do so would infringe on the rights of other residents or would not be medically advisable as documented in his medical record by the attending physician.

(24) The right to be fully informed, prior to or at the time of admission and during his stay, in writing, of the basic rate

charged by the home, of services available in the home, and of any additional charges related to such services, including charges for services not covered under Titles XVIII and XIX of the "Social Security Act," 49 Stat. 620 (1935), 42 U.S.C. 301, as amended. The basic rate shall not be changed unless thirty days notice is given to the resident or, if the resident is unable to understand this information, to his sponsor.

(25) The right of the resident and person paying for the care to examine and receive a bill at least monthly for the resident's care from the home that itemizes charges not included in the basic rates;

(26) The right to manage his personal financial affairs, or, should the home accept written delegation of this responsibility, to receive upon written request at least a quarterly accounting statement of financial transactions made on his behalf. The statement shall include:

(a) A complete record of all funds, personal property, or possessions of a resident from any source whatsoever, that have been deposited for safekeeping with the home for use by the resident or his sponsor;

(b) A listing of all deposits and withdrawals transacted, which shall be substantiated by receipts which shall be available for inspection and copying by the resident or sponsor.

(27) The right of the resident to be allowed unrestricted access to his property on deposit at reasonable hours, unless requests for access to property on deposit are so persistent, continuous, and unreasonable that they constitute a nuisance;

(28) The right not to be transferred or discharged from the home except for medical reasons, for his welfare or another resident's, for nonpayment of charges due the home, if the home's license is revoked under section 3721.03 of the Revised Code, if the home is being closed pursuant to section 5155.31 of the Revised Code, or if he is a recipient of medical assistance under section 5101.51 of the Revised Code in a home whose certification is terminated or denied under Title XVIII or XIX of the "Social Security Act," 49 Stat. 620 (1935), 42 U.S.C. 301, as amended.

(29) The right to voice grievances and recommend changes in policies and services to the home's staff, to employees of the

department of health, and to other persons not associated with the operation of the home, of the resident's choice, free from restraint, interference, coercion, discrimination, or reprisal. This right includes access to a resident's rights advocate, and the right to be a member of, to be active in, and to associate with persons who are active in organizations of relatives and friends of nursing home residents and other organizations engaged in assisting residents.

(39) The right to have any significant change in his health status reported to his sponsor. As soon as such a change is known to the home's staff, the home shall make a reasonable effort to notify the sponsor within 12 hours.

(B) A sponsor may act on a resident's behalf to assure that the home does not deny the residents' rights under sections 3721.10 to 3721.17 of the Revised Code.

(C) Any attempted waiver of the rights listed in division (A) of this section is void.[3]

Recent films on aging

The following films are available for rental from Augsburg Publishing House branches in Minneapolis (M), Columbus (C), and Los Angeles (L). Letter codes at the end of each listing indicate appropriateness for various age levels: (N) nursery, (K) kindergarten, (P) primary, (I) intermediate, (J) junior high, (S) senior high, (A) adult. An asterisk (*) following a title indicates a leader's guide is available and will be sent with the film.

Close Harmony
MCL, 30 minutes
What do 100 nine- and ten-year-olds have in common with 50 senior citizens? Love and music are combined in this Academy Award winning documentary of an intergenerational choral project in Brooklyn, N.Y.
IJSA (Learning Corporation)

Ease on Down the Road
MCL, 18 minutes
A motivational film dealing with the needs of our aging population and ways in which some church and synagogue congregations are responding. The comments and insights of the older

people and those who work with them point out that it takes just one person who cares to get things started.
SA (Franciscan)

Hello in There

M only, 21 minutes
The touching story of Mary, a widow in a boringly sterile retirement home, who mails letters to herself, shoplifts to gain attention, and visits her husband's grave for company. She is befriended by Helen, a sympathetic customer-relations representative in a department store. Their relationship develops, which eases the frustration of loneliness for the older woman and teaches the younger one much about older people.
JSA (Franciscan)

Independence and 76

MCL, 28 minutes
Jonathan, a 76-year-old widower, tries to escape the dependent life-style which he lives at the home of his affluent son. He meets Aggie, an elderly, outgoing Christian woman, whose life glows with the inner peace God can give—and his life is changed.
SA (Family Films)

Luther Metke at 94*

M only, 27 minutes
By virtue of his age and activities, Luther Metke is an exception in any generation, and an example for all. This Academy Award nominated documentary captures the essence of a spirited and lucid representative of the rural ethic at home in the Cascade Mountains of Oregon.
JSA (New Dimension Films)

The Mailbox*

MCL, 24 minutes
A moving story of an elderly woman who hopes each day to receive a letter from her children that will bring some warmth and happiness into her life.
JSA (Brigham Young)

*Peege**

MCL, 28 minutes
A well-meaning and kind family visit their blind and helpless grandmother in a nursing home. The oldest grandson tries to communicate with her by recalling shared things and good times. With a simple declaration of love, he leaves, hoping he has penetrated her dark loneliness.
JSA (Phoenix Films)

*Portrait of Grandpa Doc**

MCL, 28 minutes
As a young artist prepared for his first one-man show, he struggles to complete a portrait of his grandfather who died several years earlier. Reflecting on his childhood, he recaptures the love and encouragement of Grandpa Doc's zest for living. A sequel to *Peege*.
JSA (Pyramid)

21 Going on 70

MCL, 27 minutes
A young man, helping out at a church home for the aged, tells of his experiences as he learns to know and care about older people, listening and reacting to their challenging affirmations of Christian faith.
JSA (Outreach)

*Weekend**

M only, 10 minutes
A family of four is picnicking beneath trees in the country, but there is something not at first disclosed about the peaceful scene. Is the occasion to honor the senile old man of the family? What will this crucial day really accord him? Without words this short film achieves an ultimate irony—a poignant ending to an innocent weekend in the country.
SA (Mass Media Associates)

When Parents Grow Old*

MCL, 15-17 minutes
From *I Never Sang for My Father* with Gene Hackman and Melvyn Douglas. Theme: the problem of responsibility to aging parents and society's treatment of the elderly. A young man grapples with how to furnish care for his aging father.

You Haven't Lived Yet*

M only, 28 minutes
This positive look at aging dispels stereotypes, yet is sensitive to the realities of growing old. Real people, old and young, share both joys and sorrows of the golden years.
JSA (Better World, Inc.)

Recent films on death and dying

A Walk up the Hill*

MCL, 30 minutes
A vigorous, 77-year-old doctor, after deciding to retire, suffers a paralyzing stroke. His wife and family struggle, in the Christian faith, with the awful dilemma of whether to keep him alive—or let him die with dignity.
SA (Family Films)

Not Even Death*

MCL, 30 minutes
When Kelly's doctor tells her she has incurable cancer, she won't believe him. She's young, has two little girls, a wonderful husband, and so much to live for. In the hospital, a woman helps her understand what the Christian faith really says about death and dying.
SA (Family Films)

Happy Easter*

MCL, 30 minutes
When his grandmother dies, Davey begins to understand that death is a part of life. A film that will help children understand

that death is not the end of being, and resurrection is the promise God makes to us all. A difficult subject handled with grace and hope.
KPI (Fortress)

What Man Shall Live and Not See Death?*

MCL, 60 minutes
This film deals with the matter of death from the points of view of a patient, a bereaved wife and family, of clergy who minister to the dying, and of the doctors who are educated to preserve life. Featured are Dr. Elizabeth Kübler-Ross, eminent authority on the subject, and the Rev. Robert Neal, who conducted a seminar on death and dying at Union Theological Seminary.
SA (NBC)

Notes

Chapter 1. Myths and Realities of Aging

1. Richard Kalish, "The New Ageism and the Failure Models: A Polemic," *The Gerontologist* 19 (1979), no. 4. Reprinted in *Annual Editions: Aging* (Guilford, Conn.: Dushkin, 1983), pp. 84-88.
2. Kalish, p. 85.
3. Erdman Palmore, "Facts on Aging: A Short Quiz," *The Gerontologist* 17 (August 1977), no. 4, pp. 315-320. Reprinted in *Annual Editions: Aging* (Guilford, Conn.: Dushkin, 1980), pp. 8-13. Reprinted here by permission of *The Gerontologist/The Journal of Gerontology*.

Chapter 2. The Pilgrimage of Aging

1. Interview by Eugene C. Bianchi in *Aging as a Spiritual Journey* (New York: Crossroad, 1982), p. 241.

Chapter 3. The Tasks of Aging

1. For a more complete treatment of this, see Evelyn and James Whitehead, "Retirement," in William Clements, ed., *Ministry with the Aging* (San Francisco: Harper & Row, 1981), pp. 124-136.
2. Martin E. Marty, "Cultural Antecedents to Contemporary American Attitudes toward Aging," in Clements, pp. 56-75.
3. Bianchi, *Aging as a Spiritual Journey*, pp. 157ff.
4. Joseph Sittler, "Probing by Joseph Sittler," *The Christian Century*, September 1979, p. 157.
5. Bernice Neugarten, "Personality and the Aging Process," *The Gerontologist*, Spring 1972. Reprinted in *Annual Editions: Aging* (1980), pp. 48-52.
6. Larry Trachte, *The Meaning of Aging: Viktor Frankl's Logotherapy and the Elderly*, unpublished master's thesis, University of Iowa, 1982.

Chapter 4. The Losses and Gains of Aging

1. Paul Pruyser, "Aging: Downward, Upward or Forward?" in *Toward a Theology of Aging,* ed. Liston Mills. Special issue of *Pastoral Psychology,* 1975, pp. 102-118. The entire issue has helpful articles dealing with pastoral issues in aging.
2. Selected from John Tierney, *Esquire,* May 1982. Reprinted with permission from *Esquire,* copyright 1982 by Esquire Associates.
3. Quoted in Bianchi, *Aging as a Spiritual Journey,* p. 61.
4. Simone de Beauvoir, *Old Age* (London: Andre Deutsch, 1972), p. 6.
5. Pruyser, p. 108.
6. May Sarton, "Plant Dreaming Deep," (New York: W. W. Norton, 1983), p. 162.
7. Lee Griffin, "Gains and Losses in Aging," Unpublished paper.
8. Sarton, "Plant Dreaming Deep," p. 158.
9. Quoted in Bianchi, *Aging as a Spiritual Journey,* pp. 239-240.
10. Griffin, "Gains and Losses in Aging."
11. Ibid.
12. Quoted in Bianchi, *Aging as a Spiritual Journey,* p. 184.

Chapter 5. You Can Teach an Old Dog

1. Charlene Ager, Louise Wendt White, Wanda Mayberry, Patricia Crist, and Mary E. Conrad, "Creative Aging," *International Journal of Aging and Human Development* 1 (1980-81): 14.1. Reprinted in *Annual Editions: Aging* (1983), pp. 31-35.
2. Ibid., p. 33.
3. Paul B. Bates, K. Warner Schaie, "The Myth of the Twilight Years," *Psychology Today* (March 1974), pp. 35-38.
4. Daniel Olson, "Christian Education for Older Adults," unpublished manuscript, Minneapolis, Luther Theological Seminary, 1979, p. 5.
5. Arthur Schopenhauer.

Chapter 6. Faith Concerns of Elders

1. Bennett, John C., "Ethical Issues in Aging," in Clements, *Ministry with the Aging,* p. 229.
2. Gustav Wingren, *Luther on Vocation* (Philadelphia: Muhlenberg, 1957), pp. 70ff.
3. Martin Heinecken, in *Aging and the Older Adult* (Philadelphia: Division for Mission in North America, Lutheran Church in America, 1978), p. 17.
4. Trachte, *The Meaning of Aging,* pp. 60-61.
5. Ernest Becker, *The Denial of Death* (Glencoe, Ill.: Free Press, 1973).
6. Viktor Frankl, *Psychotherapy and Existence* (New York: Washington Square Press, 1967), p. 30.
7. Hans Schwarz, *Beyond the Gates of Death* (Minneapolis: Augsburg, 1981), esp. Chap. 5, pp. 111-133.

8. Joseph Sittler, "Conversations with Joseph Sittler," *Christian Century,* September 26, 1979, p. 917.

9. Hans Schwarz, *On the Way to the Future* (Minneapolis: Augsburg, 1980), p. 185.

10. Martin Luther, *Kritische Gesamtausgabe* (Weimar Edition of Luther's works) (Weimar: 1883ff.), vol. 22, pp. 402ff.

11. Schwarz, *On the Way to the Future,* p. 185.

Chapter 7. Faith Concerns of the Frail Elderly

1. Dorothee Soelle, *Suffering,* trans. Everett R. Kalin (Philadelphia: Fortress, 1975), pp. 70-78.

2. John A. T. Robinson, *Exploration into God* (Stanford: Stanford Univ., 1967), pp. 68-73, 94-96.

3. Albert Outler, *Who Trusts in God* (New York: Oxford, 1968).

Chapter 8. Ethical Issues in Aging

1. John C. Bennett, "Ethical Aspects of Aging in America," p. 138.

2. Ibid., p. 139.

3. Martin Heinecken, "A Lot to Be Done," *Lutheran Standard,* March 1979.

Chapter 9. Facing the Dilemmas of Dying

1. Albert Outler, autobiographical statement quoted in Bianchi, *Aging as a Spiritual Journey,* p. 245.

2. Vincent A. Yzermans, *The Major Addresses of Pope Pius XII* (St. Paul, North Central, 1981), p. 401. See also James B. Nelson, *Human Medicine* (Minneapolis: Augsburg, 1984), Chap. 6, pp. 142-175.

3. Daniel E. Lee, *Death and Dying: Ethical Choices in a Caring Community* (Philadelphia: Division for Mission in North America, Lutheran Church in America, 1983).

4. John C. Bennett, "The Van Dusens Suicide Pact," *Christianity and Crisis,* March 1975, pp. 66-68.

5. Dietrich Bonhoeffer, *Ethics* (New York: Macmillan, 1955), p. 168.

6. Stanley Heuerwas, *Truthfulness and Tragedy* (Notre Dame; Univ. of Notre Dame, 1977); see pp. 112-113. The entire Chap. 6, "Memory, Community and the Reasons for Living: Reflections on Suicide and Euthanasia" (pp. 101-115), is very informative.

Chapter 10. Pastoral Counseling with Elders

1. See my book *The Compassionate Visitor* (Minneapolis: Augsburg, 1984). In my judgment the foundation of all pastoral care is compassion. A detailed treatment of the nature and dynamics of compassion is contained in that volume and also in the *Trinity Seminary Review* 5 (Spring 1983), no. 1, pp. 14-21.

2. Barry Estadt, *Pastoral Counseling* (Englewood Cliffs, N.J.: Prentice-Hall, 1983), pp. 132-133.

3. An argument has been going on for some time as to whether a parish pastor can, or ought, to do any intensive counseling. There are valid points on both sides of the question. Much hinges on how "intensive counseling" is defined. Generally I contend that, for the average parish pastor with good seminary training in pastoral care (including a unit or two of C.P.E.), counseling as part of normal parish duties with a specific individual should probably not exceed six to ten hour-long sessions.

4. Excellent resources for pastoral crisis counseling are now available. An annotated bibliography for pastoral care has been prepared by the Division for Theological Education and Ministry of the American Lutheran Church. I find David K. Switzer, *The Minister as Crisis Counselor* (Nashville: Abingdon, 1974) very helpful. See also Gerald Kennedy, *Crisis Counseling* (New York: Continuum, 1981); Howard Stone, *Crisis Counseling* (Philadelphia: Fortress, 1976); Howard J. Parad, *Crisis Intervention* (Family Service Association of America, 1965).

5. See her helpful chapter, "The Ministry of Crisis Intervention," in Estadt, *Pastoral Counseling.*

6. An excellent outline for this type of counseling can be found in Patricia Alpaugh and Margaret Haney, *Counseling the Older Adult: A Training Manual for Paraprofessional and Beginning Counselors* (San Diego: Univ. of Southern Calif., 1978).

7. The literature in family therapy is quite extensive. Here we can only highlight a few of the volumes especially useful to the pastor. A classic in the field is Virginia Satir, *Conjoint Family Therapy: A Guide to Theory and Technique* (Palo Alto, Calif.: Science and Behavior, 1967). See also J. C. Wynn, *Family Therapy in Pastoral Ministry* (San Francisco: Harper & Row, 1972).

8. Albert Meiburg, "Pastoral Communication with the Confused," *Pastoral Psychology* 31 (Summer 1983). Reprinted with permission from *Pastoral Psychology*, copyright 1983 by Human Sciences Press.

9. M. Skelly, "Aphasic Patients Talk Back," *American Journal of Nursing*, July 1975, pp. 1140-1142.

10. Adrian Verwoerdt, "Individual Psychotherapy on Senile Dementia," *Aging* 15 (1981). Reprinted in Nancy E. Miller and Gene D. Cohen, eds., *Clinical Aspects of Alzheimer's Disease and Senile Dementia* (New York: Raven, 1981), pp. 187-207.

Chapter 11. Family Counseling with Elders

1. See Virginia Satir, *Conjoint Family Therapy;* Ronald F. Levant, *Family Therapy: A Comprehensive Overview* (Englewood Cliffs, N.J.: Prentice-Hall, 1984) has a very good review of the current concepts and state of family counseling.

2. John J. Herr and John H. Weakland, *Counseling Elders and Their Families* (New York: Springer, 1979). Copyright © 1979 Springer Publishing Company. Used by permission. The full, detailed case of Mrs. C. is found in Chapter 14.

Chapter 12. The Local Congregation Ministers to Elders

1. Thomas Oden, *Pastoral Theology* (San Francisco, Harper and Row, 1983), p. 26.
2. Arthur H. Becker, *The Compassionate Visitor* (Minneapolis: Augsburg, 1984).
3. Elisabeth Kübler-Ross, *On Death and Dying* (New York: Macmillan, 1969).

Appendix

1. The inventory on attitudes on aging is reprinted with permission of Ontario Department of Social and Family Services, Windsor, Ontario.
2. This bill of rights was created at a workshop on "The Terminally Ill Patient and the Helping Person," in Lansing, Michigan, sponsored by the Southwestern Michigan Inservice Education Council and conducted by Amelia J. Barbus, former associate professor of nursing, Wayne State University, Detroit, and is reprinted by permission.
3. The bill of rights is from Section 3721.13 of the Amended House Bill #600, enacted by the General Assembly of the State of Ohio. Similar legislation has been enacted by many other states.

Selected Bibliography

The literature on aging is extensive, so there is no attempt here to offer a complete bibliography. Included in this list are resources that in my opinion are particularly useful to pastors and congregations.

Becker, Arthur H. *The Compassionate Visitor*. Minneapolis: Augsburg, 1985.

Bianchi, Eugene C. *Aging as a Spiritual Journey*. New York: Crossroad, 1982.

Birren, James E. *The Psychology of Aging*. Englewood Cliffs, N.J.: Prentice-Hall, 1964.

Butler, R. N., and Lewis, M. E. *Love and Sex after Sixty: A Guide for Men and Women in Their Later Years*. New York: Harper & Row, 1977.

Butler, Robert N. *Why Survive? Being Old in America*. New York: Harper & Row, 1975.

Clements, William M. *Care and Counseling of the Aging*. Philadelphia: Fortress, 1979.

Clements, William M., ed. *Ministry with the Aging*. San Francisco: Harper & Row, 1983.

Cusack, Odean, and Smith, Elaine. *Pets and the Elderly: The Therapeutic Bond*. New York: Haworth, 1984.

Datan, Nancy, and Lohmann, Nancy, eds. *Transitions of Aging*. New York: Academic, 1980.

Gillies, John. *A Guide to Caring for and Coping with Aging Parents*. Nashville: Thomas Nelson, 1981.

Herr, John J., and Weakland, John H. *Counseling Elders and Their Families*. New York: Springer, 1979.

Hussian, Richard A. *Geriatric Psychology: A Behavioral Perspective.* New York: Van Nostrand Reinhold, 1981.

Kübler-Ross, Elisabeth. *On Death and Dying.* New York: Macmillan, 1969.

Levinson, Daniel J., et al. *The Seasons of a Man's Life.* New York: Knopf, 1978.

Maves, Paul B. *A Place to Live in Your Later Years.* Religion and Medicine Series. Minneapolis: Augsburg, 1983.

Maves, Paul B. *Faith for the Older Years.* Minneapolis: Augsburg, 1986.

McGill, Arthur C. *Suffering: A Test of Theological Method.* Philadelphia: Westminster, 1982.

Meiburg, Albert. "Pastoral Communication with the Confused." *Pastoral Psychology* 31 (Summer 1983): 271-281.

Neugarten, Bernice L., ed. *Middle Age and Aging: A Reader in Social Psychology.* Chicago: University of Chicago, 1968.

Pelgrin, Mark. *And a Time to Die.* Eds. Sheila Moon and Elizabeth Howes. Wheaton, Ill.: Theosophical, 1976.

Rogers, Dorothy. *The Adult Years: An Introduction to Aging.* 2nd ed. Englewood Cliffs, N.J.: Prentice-Hall, 1982.

Schlossberg, Nancy, et al. *Perspectives on Counseling Adults: Issues and Skills.* Monterey, Calif.: Wadsworth, 1983.

Schwarz, Hans. *On the Way to the Future.* Minneapolis: Augsburg, 1979.

Schwarz, Hans. *Beyond the Gates of Death.* Minneapolis: Augsburg, 1981.

Smith, Bert Kruger. *Aging in America.* Boston: Beacon, 1973.

Stagg, Frederick. *The Bible Speaks on Aging.* Nashville: Broadman, 1981.

Tillberg, Cedric, ed. *Aging and the Older Adult.* Philadelphia: Division of Mission in America, Lutheran Church in America.

Tillberg, Cedric W. *Revolution Underway: An Aging Church in an Aging Society.* Philadelphia: Fortress, 1984.

Trachte, Larry. *The Meaning of Aging: Viktor Frankl's Logotherapy and the Elderly.* M.A. Thesis. University of Iowa, 1982.

Trickman, G. "Caring for the Confused or Delirious Patient." *American Journal of Nursing* 78 (September 1978): 1496.

Verwoerdt, Adrian. "Individual Psychotherapy in Senile Dementia." *Aging: 15* Clinical Aspects of Alzheimer's Disease and Senile Dementia. Ed. Nancy E. Miller and Gene D. Cohen. New York: Raven, 1981.

Wynn, John C. *Family Therapy in Pastoral Ministry.* San Francisco: Harper & Row, 1982.